MARVELOUSLY *Made*

I know few women, if any, who can't identify with the issues Monica covers in *Marvelously Made*. The message of being real and truly seeking identity through Christ is timely and essential, especially considering what women are up against in our culture. Monica's transparency with her own struggles as well as the biblical path she points women to follow will help many drop their masks to take hold of how marvelously God has created them!

CHRIS ADAMS
Senior Lead Women's Ministry Specialist, Nashville, Tennessee

If you're tired of pretending or have ever struggled with the vulnerability of being real with God, yourself and others, *Marvelously Made* is just the book for you. Monica shares openly from her own personal experience and biblical insight to inspire women to remove their own phony masks and reveal their true identity and purpose through the uniqueness of who they are in Christ.

TAMMY BENNETT
Author, *101 MakeOver Minutes: Quick Tips for Looking Good from the Inside Out*
Women's Ministry Strategist, Southern Baptist Conservatives of Virginia
Glen Allen, Virginia

Marvelously Made is a must read! Monica Brennan takes women on a journey of discovering the beauty and fulfillment of living by God's unique design. She helps women see how they can take off their masks and find their *true identity* in Christ. This book will encourage you and inspire you to discover healing through authentic living.

LISA HARRINGTON BRYANT
Women's Ministry Director, Thomas Road Baptist Church, Lynchburg, Virginia

Once the self-described "Queen of Masquerades," Monica Brennan has discovered the freedom and joy of taking off the masks and walking in her true identity in Christ. *Marvelously Made* gets to the heart of the issues that keep so many women in bondage. I am confident this book will help women—young and older—enter into a greater experience of life as God intended it to be!

NANCY LEIGH DEMOSS
Author of *Revive Our Hearts* and radio teacher/host

Monica Brennan has been used in the lives of countless women by helping them discover the same truths that set her free many years ago. Years of pouring out this message of freedom have finally culminated in this must-read book. You are in for rich biblical truth and the blessing of hearing from one of God's most anointed servants in this generation!

MEREDITH FLOYD
Director of Women's Ministry, Cross Church, Fayetteville, Arkansas

Marvelously Made is a real treasure for women of all ages. Monica Rose Brennan has written a practical and purposeful book to help women understand who they truly are in Christ. We all need to hear this truth supported by Scripture that she presents so profoundly, and this is a book that can be read and re-read throughout our lives. Monica shares it with such a soft heart that comes from her relationship with our Lord and the experiences He has walked through with her. I highly recommend it to every woman as they grow in their spiritual walk.

LYNNE GAGE
Administrator and 4G Girls Retreat Leader, Go Tell Ministries, Duluth, Georgia

Marvelously Made is a beautiful depiction of God's intent when making us. The relevance and practicality in the pages make it a must-read for all women.

AUTUMN MILES
Founder and President, The Blush Network

We live in a world of makeup and makeovers, of cosmetic surgery and an obsession with outward appearance. In *Marvelously Made,* Monica Rose Brennan challenges the perception of plastic and surface with a God-centered, inward understanding of beauty and worth. Biblical truth and personal stories converge as Monica offers a remarkable portrait of a woman whose hope is in Christ, not the idols we create. Read this book and enjoy the acceptance you have in Jesus!

ALVIN L. REID
Professor of Evangelism and Student Ministry/Bailey Smith Chair of Evangelism
Southeastern Baptist Theological Seminary, Wake Forest, North Carolina

I first met Monica Rose Brennan when she was a student at Liberty Baptist Theological Seminary. I challenged her to get her education—all the way to a doctorate degree. She did, and today she is the chairman of the women's ministry division at Liberty University. *Marvelously Made* is about everything that Monica Rose Brennan has become. What Monica communicates to the young women at Liberty University she communicates to readers in this book, and I know it will transform the lives of those who read it. I recommend *Marvelously Made* with enthusiasm.

ELMER L. TOWNS
Co-founder, Liberty University
Dean, Liberty Baptist Theological Seminary and Graduate School, Lynchburg, Virginia

MONICA ROSE BRENNAN

MARVELOUSLY *Made*

UNVEIL YOUR TRUE IDENTITY AND PURPOSE AS A WOMAN

Regal

For more information and
special offers from Regal Books, email us at
subscribe@regalbooks.com

Published by Regal
From Gospel Light
Ventura, California, U.S.A.
www.regalbooks.com
Printed in the U.S.A.

Library of Congress Cataloging-in-Publication Data
Brennan, Monica Rose.
Marvelously made : unveil your true identity & purpose as a woman /
Monica Rose Brennan.
p. cm.
Includes bibliographical references (p.   ) and index.
ISBN 978-0-8307-6415-0 (trade paper : alk. paper)
1. Christian women—Religious life. I. Title.
BV4527.B6845 2012
248.8'43—dc23
2012006439

Rights for publishing this book outside the U.S.A. or in non-English languages are
administered by Gospel Light Worldwide, an international not-for-profit ministry.
For additional information, please visit www.glww.org, email info@glww.org, or write
to Gospel Light Worldwide, 1957 Eastman Avenue, Ventura, CA 93003, U.S.A.

To order copies of this book and other Regal products in bulk quantities,
please contact us at 1-800-446-7735.

Dedicated to my daughter:
Elizabeth Rose Brennan, my precious gift from God.

You have been with me, either inside my womb or outside my womb,
as I completed this book. The Lord constantly reminded me of how
uniquely He was creating you as I would feel you move inside of me.
I still had one more chapter to complete before you were born,
but to our surprise you arrived two weeks earlier than expected.
Once again, the Lord reminded me of His
perfect timing for your arrival.

I wondered how I could complete the book with all of my thoughts being
on you and you alone. I became so fascinated by your tiny hand that
would wrap around my finger and your barely open eyes as they
looked up into my face for the very first time. The more enamored I
became with you, the more passionate I became with what the Lord had
burdened my heart to put into words. The Lord used you as a constant
inspiration to complete what He had placed on my heart.

My precious daughter: You are marvelously made! I look forward to
seeing all the many purposes Christ has for your life.
I pray that you will discover more fully who He is every day and
as a result know who you are as His daughter. May you radiate His
image before others and live out His unchanging Truths
that will never fail you! I love you forever.

Love, Mother

I will praise You, for I am fearfully and wonderfully made.
PSALM 139:14

Contents

MARVELOUSLY
Made

Foreword

I have been traveling and speaking to women for three decades, and I have never met anyone like Dr. Monica Rose Brennan. What sets her apart from thousands of women that I have met during my traveling is her incomparable passion for inspiring God's girls to discover God's best for them. Coupled with her passion is a deep wisdom that allows her to guide women—young and old—to discover their most noble life purpose. Monica knows personally that a woman's deepest joy comes from discovering the very purpose for which she was created and born again.

Now, in *Marvelously Made*, Dr. Brennan has put her heart's wisdom in print. Every page of this book has been lived and taught and edited by life experience. Dr. Brennan is not writing from textbook research but from life experience—she has personally wrestled with the very things she writes about that rob a woman of her true identity. She has grasped the reality of the "opaque veil" that hides the face of God from the soul of His girls. She has discovered in God's Word the principles that set women free—free to glorify God in their everyday lives.

> *Self is the opaque veil that hides the face of God*
> *from us. It can be removed only in spiritual experience,*
> *never by mere instruction.*
> A. W. TOZER

The chapters in this book will provide a spiritual experience that will allow you to pull back the "opaque veil" and reveal your true identity. When you get a glimpse of this true identity, the veil will be pulled back far enough that you will have a glimpse of God's noble purpose for your life. Dr. Brennan knows that a true self-worth is the result of knowing God's truth about a woman—nothing more, but nothing less. As the "opaque veil" is pulled back with each page, you will discover the freedom that God's truth brings to the soul.

Marvelously Made is a twenty-first century guidebook that will help you discover with clarity God's noble purpose for your life. The questions at the end of each chapter will help keep the veil pulled back as you proceed from one chapter to another. Now begin your journey in pulling back the "opaque veil."

Jackie Kendall
Bestselling Author of *Lady in Waiting*
President of Power to Grow, Inc.

Identity Unmasked

*Behold, you delight in truth in the inward being,
and you teach me wisdom in the secret heart.*
PSALM 51:6, *ESV*

*We can never know who or what we are till we
know at least something of what God is.*
A. W. TOZER

*It is a great thing when I discover I am no
longer my own, but His.*
WATCHMAN NEE

CHAPTER ONE

What Does It Mean to Be Real?

And you shall know the truth, and the truth shall make you free.
JOHN 8:32

Behold, You desire truth in the inward parts, and in the hidden part You will make me to know wisdom.
PSALM 51:6

When I was a little girl, my favorite thing was to play with my Barbie dolls. After every school day and during every weekend, I would run straight to my room and pull a large case out from under my bed. I would sit on the floor for hours creating a story for each of my Barbie dolls. I was *the creator* of each personality as well as *the author* of each unique life. Each Barbie doll had been given a name, personality and role to play in my world of imagination. This world was created by me and for me, so I enjoyed it immensely.

My Barbie doll world would increase in number after my birthday and Christmas. In fact, my Barbie world could never get too big; there was always room to add another member of the family and give her a name, personality and role to play that was different from any of the others.

As "the designer" of my Barbie world, I would usually play by myself. Of course, the fact that I was growing up with two mischievous brothers demanded that it be that way; on more than one occasion, I found both of them in my room, cutting off my dolls' heads, hair or arms. This always resulted in a tragic and devastating day for me (and for my Barbie dolls, to say the least). Although I played alone most of the time, I preferred it that way. When other girls came over to play with me, they would want to give my Barbie dolls different names, personalities and roles than the ones I had given them.

As you can tell, I took my Barbie world seriously. Indeed, it was so serious to me that I had unconsciously made this make-believe world a reality . . . at least in my six-year-old mind. For this was the world created by me and for me, and I didn't want anyone to mess it up. Each story I made up for my Barbie dolls to play was built upon another story. Although anyone else would look at my Barbie world as *pretend*, it became very *real* to me.

Echoes from the Garden

Why did I love this imaginary world so much? In my Barbie world there was always laughter. When Barbie and Ken got in a fight, they always kissed and made up, and life was amazingly great once again. In my Barbie world, there were countless birthday parties, weddings, celebrations and adventures.

Each Barbie doll fell in love with a Ken doll and never suffered from insecurities, fears or rejections. They would date for a while, and shortly after their engagement have a beautiful wedding. I used a roll of toilet tissue as the runner down the middle of the aisle for the bride's grand entrance. In my Barbie world, everyone wanted the bride and groom to be married, so the wedding was never interrupted by a runaway bride or frazzled in-laws. There were no breakups or hurt feelings, only love and acceptance. And the love they experienced was unconditional.

Ken never thought of anyone other than Barbie, and Barbie never wished for anyone other than Ken. Shortly after marriage, Barbie and Ken had children they equally desired and cared for. There was never abuse, neglect, hate or rejection.

There was never lasting pain in the world I created. No one ever felt alone, hurt, abandoned, hopeless, depressed, anxious or overwhelmed. Everything and anything I created for my Barbie world only brought joy.

None of my Barbie dolls saw themselves as a mistake or an accident. Each one had a place to belong. There was always adventure—from water parks to camp-outs in Barbie's camper or long travels to exotic destinations in Barbie's airplane. It was a great world to be in, and I enjoyed creating it immensely!

The only story I didn't create for my Barbie dolls to experience was death. No one ever died in my Barbie doll world. I honestly never remember having one single thought of any of my Barbie dolls dying. Thus, there were never any funerals. There was no thought of loss and no uncertainty about eternity.

Emotionally speaking, everything was absolutely perfect in the world created by me and for me. No one was ever rejected. No one was insecure, worried, overweight, underweight, ugly, lonely or afraid. There was no depression, disease or disorder. No phobias, abuse, divorce, cutting or suicide attempts. The only things that existed in the world created by me and for me were the extreme opposites of reality.

Although the world I created at a very young age was a "utopia," it was pretend. The world in which I truly lived was the opposite of the one I had created. In fact, all the worlds of escape or pretend that we create in our imagination are the opposite of the world in which we live. We all know of the realities of the world in which we were born, regardless of how hard we seek to escape from sickness, conflicts, pain . . . death.

Sounds from the Real World

While growing up as a pastor's daughter, I went to countless funeral services. In fact, I grew up living in a parsonage, with the church on one side and the cemetery on the other. I heard thousands of messages on the sinful world in which we were born. Each day of my life I overheard conversations regarding difficulties people were going through, from alcohol abuse to physical, verbal and emotional abuse of women. Many times, people would show up at my house, the parsonage, with no place to stay and no reason to live . . . completely homeless and hopeless, trying to find money, often for their next "fix." I also heard innumerable sermons on the reality of heaven and hell, on life and death.

With messages like these in my mind, growing up, I would frequently escape into my utopia world of pretend. I would tell myself that I was okay and everyone else was okay and everything was going to work out, although I had no clue where I personally was going to spend eternity. Thoughts of death frightened me. I escaped to a shelter made by me and for me as often as I could, which was every day. In fact, I preferred my pretend shelter to the world of reality on any given day. Reality wasn't fun.

If you think I had an imagination in my Barbie world, then you wouldn't be surprised to learn that I also had an imaginary friend named Sasha. Sasha came into my life when I was four years old and didn't leave until I was seven. I would talk to her just like she was standing right beside me. We had tea parties, birthday parties for my Cabbage Patch Kids, and celebrations for no reason at all. Sasha was a great friend because she was always there when I wanted her to be; and when I didn't want her around, she would leave. Sasha would do everything I told her to do and anything I wanted to do, so we had a perfect friendship. Again, I preferred my world of pretend to reality any day!

Creating a Grown-Up Pretend World

Now, I am an adult woman. I no longer play with my Barbie dolls for hours at a time on the floor. I also no longer have an imaginary friend. I no longer live in my world of pretend, at least not in my Barbie world. However, for some reason, when someone asks me how I'm doing, I almost always escape into my world of pretend just as I did when I was a little girl . . . *I lie.* "Doing great! And how are you?" "Wonderful, just wonderful, great day, isn't it?"

Deep inside I am hurting, fearful, anxious, insecure, lonely and confused. I feel plastic, artificial, lost. However, I wouldn't dare tell anyone. In fact, you probably wouldn't either, because the majority of us prefer the world of pretend to the world of reality. It's almost as if even when we are very young we prefer a world that doesn't exist over reality, even though at age four, reality isn't all that bad! Think about it . . . we have our needs met, someone to take care of us . . . we don't even have to think for ourselves. Yet, *we still want to escape from the world we are in and become someone we are not.*

What did you want to be when you were a little girl? Your world of imagination may have changed on a daily or weekly basis—from dreaming of being Cinderella or Wonder Woman or a little kitty cat; and almost every little girl dreams of being a bride one day. But why wait, right? Embrace the world of pretend and you can be walking down the aisle in seconds!

I remember so vividly the words, "Sir, you may kiss your bride." These words were spoken to the groom who was pretending to be my groom when I was seven years old. I was not officially married at age seven, but in my make-believe world, I most assuredly was! My brother Brady was the preacher, pronouncing me and my other brother, Jeremy, as husband and wife. (And, yes, I am from the South!) Brady, who was four years old at the time, had managed to put on one of my father's black suit coats and carried in his little arms our family Bible. Jeremy had on my father's full attire—pants, suit coat, tie and shoes. I had arranged the entire event. My brothers were too young to know any better, but they still remember this very organized and well-thought-out event to this very day! I had a long cloth over my head that served as a veil and my own beautiful white lacy dress. I remember playing in this make-believe world of mine countless times.

Everything in my pretend land happened the way I wanted it to happen. I was in control over everything, just as I was in control of my Barbie world. Others who played with me were in control of their roles as well. However, I was not the only one with an imagination. When outdoors, my brothers played cowboys and Indians, and I was the girl they had to protect except when we played superheroes and I was Wonder Woman or G. I. Jane.

Did you ever believe your Barbie dolls or stuffed animals came to life when you went to bed? I honestly believed they did! I remember that before getting into bed each night, I would turn off the lights really fast and then cut them back on to see if any of my dolls had moved. This false reality was so much fun to believe in! I began to prefer the world of pretend over reality.

No one has to teach us to pretend, do they? It comes so naturally. Perhaps when we dress up on Halloween we are simply being honest with how we feel for the other 364 days in the year. *We wear masks.* I am not suggesting that we never should use our imagination or that we never should read fiction or watch unrealistic movies; but what I am in hopes of your considering is *the danger of living an entire life in pretend mode and never coming to a place of reality where you ask yourself the question, "What does it mean to be real?"*

What Does It Mean to Be Real?

Do you remember the story of *The Velveteen Rabbit*? A stuffed little bunny became a young boy's favorite Christmas present one year and became his most beloved stuffed animal. He took it everywhere he went and slept with it at night. As the boy grew older, he didn't play with the stuffed bunny all that much and the other toys would even make fun of the velveteen rabbit. One day the stuffed bunny asked the toy horse, "What is real? Does it mean having batteries or lights?" "Real isn't how you are made," said the Play Horse. "It's a thing that happens to you. When a child really loves you, that is when you become Real."[1]

Although the story of *The Velveteen Rabbit* is fictional children's literature, it holds a lot of truth about the meaning of "real." *What must happen to us for us to become "real"?* What is it that we must discover in order to know our true identity and keep us from escaping and living in our world of pretend for our entire life?

Not only are we born into a world where it is natural to pretend, but we are also inclined to prefer this pretend world, using our imagination even when we grow up, because, all too often, the reality of the world in which we live is too painful. Are you with me? Have you ever asked yourself these questions?

- Who wants to live in a world where there is pain?
- Who wants to live in a world of rejection, insecurities, fears and conflicts?
- Who wants to live in a world of death?
- Is there a way of escape?

Today when I look back at my childhood and the make-believe kingdoms I so creatively designed, and I ponder the wonderful world of my imagination, I want to go back to that place. In reality, I go back there a lot. I imagine a safe, secure place where everything is the way I think it should be . . . a place where I know who I am . . . a place where I feel wanted, accepted, secure and loved. *Do you ever find yourself in that place too?*

Our thoughts, imagination and fantasies take us to places we want so desperately to belong to, because we don't feel like we fit where we are. We are discontent and dissatisfied with all the "who," "what" and "where." It's much easier to create our little world of pretend and wear a mask. We drift to this safe place a lot, don't we? Life is better in our make-believe lands. We are happier in a world controlled by self.

The Discomfort of the Reality

Reality is not pretend; it is the everyday life that we wake up to each morning. When we find ourselves unfulfilled with an un-remarkable existence, we often take our pretend land that we have been thinking of for so long and say, "There has to be a way out of reality and a way to get to the world I've created—a world of happiness."

Now, even though we have thoughts like these rather con-sistently, we still wake up each and every morning to the real. We feel pain caused by rejection; deep-rooted bitterness because someone has deeply hurt us; unhealed wounds that lay open to other infections because they have never been treated; conflicts in key relationships; discontentment with who we are; a lack of fulfillment in what we do; confusion with the here and now; dis-appointment in our own behavior and the unfairness of life; questions in regard to why we are here; the feeling of not belong-ing to anyone; a deep desire to be loved; mixed feelings about the future; fear of failure; thoughts of insignificance . . .

We are not comfortable in a world we don't feel at home in, with people who seem so unrelated. We often feel stuck in some-one else's frame, screaming out, "Where am I, and how did I get to this place of such confusion?" It's so much easier to simply pretend that everything is okay and not allow our thoughts to take us to the pain we are experiencing. At times we hold things in—we don't speak of our discontentment, insecurities and con-fusion with anyone. At times we lose control and attack the ones who are the closest to us and say things we never thought would come out of our mouths.

We pretend. Why? Because we feel more comfortable being someone we are not and because we are clueless as to who we really are and why we were created. And let's face it, we are happy in a world that doesn't exist, happy pretending to be someone we are not, happy being plastic ... fake ... paper dolls. Or are we really pretending to be "happy" because we are so confused that we lose hope of ever finding the answers we so desperately desire to have answered ... the questions we find so difficult to ask ... the one question we wrestle with: *Who am I?* Instead of seeking the answer to who we are, we unconsciously escape to a place of pretend. We enter into the world as natural pretenders.

We imagine, we hope and we dream of far-off places; we are "pretend people" who run into our secret rooms, discontent with the real and unable to understand fully who we are. We often find someone we can imitate or we seek to become someone we are not. We live in a world full of imitation, so it is extremely easy to find someone to follow—to be like, to act like, to dress like, to talk like. We have no identity of our own, so we try to fit the mold of someone else.

No Masks

The problem with being *censored* (molded into someone else's frame) is that we were never created to wear a mask. In other words, you were never created to have a false identity or to live in a land of pretend. Did you hear that? *We were never created to wear a mask and have a false identity.* If we never realize whose we are (our identity) and to whom we belong (our security) and why we are here (our destiny), we will never know the freedom and joy of embracing our identity unmasked (who we really are and were created to be).

If we live our entire lives pretending and not understanding who our Creator has made us to be, we will miss finding out the reason we were created . . . the reason we exist! We will have many difficulties in our relationships—with our Maker, ourselves and with others. I don't know about you, but I want to know who I am. I want and need to know to whom I belong. I desperately need to know why I am here on planet Earth! Don't you?

Remember the movie *Runaway Bride*, produced in 1999? Julia Roberts plays the role of Maggie Carpenter, engaged to be married, who is known for having left many a fiancé at the altar. Richard Gere plays the role of Ike Graham, a reporter who is writing a story about the "Runaway Bride." In the process of writing the story, Ike finds himself falling in love with Maggie, but she eventually leaves him at the altar too. Throughout Ike and Maggie's relationship, Ike points out on many occasions the fact that Maggie doesn't really know who she is. He brings up the fact that she "blends in" with whatever type of guy she is with, including his likes and dislikes. Ike even discusses with Maggie that she doesn't even know how she likes her eggs cooked. She simply likes her eggs prepared in whatever manner the guy she is engaged to likes his. This forces Maggie into deep thought. She eventually discovers who she is by choosing not to be identified solely by blending in with whoever she is with or by what others like or dislike.

Before we actually come to the reality of who we are, we often unintentionally choose to keep pretending to be someone we are not, just like Maggie Carpenter.

Has anyone ever asked you how you were doing and how your day was and *you lied* about it? I have lied on many occasions when others have asked me questions in regard to how I am doing. Just as I often lie about "reality," I'm convinced that most of us do the same. In fact, reality hurts so badly that we would rather live in the world of pretend. The tragic thing is that the world of pretend becomes so consistent in our lives that we spend most of our time not ever realizing we are pretending. *The masks we wear begin to feel so comfortable that we no longer see them as masks, but as reality,* just as I believed my Barbie world was real when I was a little girl.

Do You Really Want to Pretend?

Although pretend feels very good and provides a quick way of escape, you are not ready to truly live until you are ready to face reality. It is impossible to embrace your true identity apart from coming to grips with "true reality." So, the question is the same question that the Velveteen Rabbit asked the toy rocking horse: "What does it mean to be REAL?"

By definition, "real" means "being or occurring in fact or actuality; having verifiable existence, true and actual; not imaginary, alleged, or ideal, genuine and authentic; not artificial or spurious, being no less than what is stated; worthy of the name, free of pretense, falsehood, or affectation, not to be taken lightly; serious."[2] Some synonyms for "real" are "actual, true, existent." The "real" that we are discussing is "not imaginary—existing as fact, rather than as a product of dreams or the imagination."[3]

Artificial ingredients are everywhere and usually come from the desperate desire for instant gratification. The first time I had instant potatoes was when I was a freshman in college. I grew up with my mother teaching me to cook with *real* ingredients. It was a very rare event if we used anything instant in our cooking. I grew up in the country—the mountains of North Carolina to be exact. Most every year my parents grew their own vegetables; and if they didn't, my Uncle Joe and Uncle Ned would load us up with bags full of nature's best! So it just made sense to use the real stuff!

A friend of mine in college grew up in the big city, and both of her parents worked outside the home. Everything she ate was almost always instant. She came home with me one weekend and tasted real mashed potatoes for the first time. Although they were real, the mashed potatoes didn't taste good to her. Can you believe that? She had become so accustomed to the artificial potatoes that she thought something was wrong with the real. So often we live in pretend for so long that we become completely oblivious to the fact that we don't know who we are. This is an extremely scary place to be—unaware that you are living a lie.

Live Real

We live in a society of pretenders . . . masquerades . . . fakes . . . plastics . . . artificial ingredients . . . paper dolls . . . trying to look real because the "real" is what we are all looking for and wanting to be. Would you agree? It's interesting that the majority of single women I talk to say that one of the top qualities they look for in a potential dating partner is honesty. So often break-ups occur when we discover the person we really cared for was dishonest, wearing a mask, pretending to be someone he was not. This causes a lot of pain and tears.

Think about how it makes our Creator feel when we are dishonest with Him. The interesting thing about God is that He is always aware when we are hiding from Him and wearing a mask. His love is so deep that no matter how deep the layers of our masks become, He still desperately desires to know us and for us to know Him. Psalm 51:6 reveals the heart of God. The psalmist declares, "Behold, you delight in truth in the inward being, and you teach me wisdom in the secret heart" (ESV). Our Maker delights in truth. Our Creator desires us to be real with Him and He has promised to teach us wisdom.

Would you agree with me that honesty is what we want from others and from ourselves? We want to be real, and we desperately desire others to be real with us—about who we are and who we were created to be. Regardless of our past hurts or confusion, God has a plan. He desires that you know Him for who He is and embrace who He has created you to be. You are accepted and loved by the Creator of the heavens and the earth: He is your Maker.

I will never forget when a young lady approached me after class one day and said with intensity, "I am not ready to meet with you, but I know I need to . . . I am not ready to come to grips with my issues." I had just taught a lesson on being real with God.

Has fear ever paralyzed you from facing the truth? We are often afraid to be honest about some of our experiences; wrong choices, tragedies that hurt us, blame, guilt and shame keep us imprisoned from ever experiencing the freedom Christ desires us to embrace. In order to more fully understand who we are and why we were created, we must first be truthful.

Remember the opposite of being real? It's wearing a mask and pretending everything is all right even though deep inside we know it is not. This was how my dear friend was living. Several weeks after the young lady approached me after class, she came by my office and began to share some of the issues she had been battling with for years: resentment, hurt, bitterness and shame. As I listened to her, all I could think of was the fact that she was being genuine. She was being authentic with herself and with God, her Creator.

When I shared with her how she was loved and accepted by Christ and how He desired her to have freedom to know Him on a deeper level, tears began to run down her cheeks and a faint smile appeared. She was finally able to begin answering the question: *Who am I?* The mask was coming off. Jesus said, "And you shall know the truth, and the truth shall make you free" (John 8:32). What is truth? Jesus testifies in John 14:6, "I am the way, the truth, and the life. No one comes to the Father except through Me." Jesus Christ is the truth, and when you place your trust in Him, you will experience the joy of knowing Him, understanding more fully who you are, and embracing His destiny for your life.

We spend so much of our time pretending that everything is okay; yet, it is only when we are real with who we are and who God is that He will be able to be real with us. Remember what the psalmist David declared in Psalm 51:6: "Behold, you delight in truth in the inward being, and you teach me wisdom in the secret heart" (*ESV*). God wants us to be real. We can start by being honest about our thoughts toward Him, good or bad. He knows them anyway.

I remember going through some of the darkest days of my life while in college. I didn't "feel" God at all. In fact, God felt so distant. It seemed as if He didn't care about me anymore. Then I began to be honest with Him and pour out my heart. It was in my moments of complete authenticity with my Maker, my

Creator God, that He made Himself known to me in a greater way than I had ever experienced or imagined.

Remember the story of Hannah in 1 Samuel 1–2? We learn all sorts of details about this remarkable woman of faith. Hannah was married to a man named Elkanah, who actually had another wife named Peninnah. Although Elkanah had two wives, he loved Hannah, although she was barren. Peninnah was cruel to Hannah, probably due to this fact, and would constantly remind her of her barrenness: "And her rival used to provoke her grievously to irritate her, because the LORD had closed her womb" (1 Sam. 1:6, *ESV*). You can probably imagine why Hannah had such a great desire to give birth.

Although Hannah was a woman of faith, her faith was not developed until she approached the Lord with an authentic heart. Hannah became so distressed that she stopped eating and could only weep: "She was deeply distressed and prayed to the LORD and wept bitterly. And she vowed a vow and said, 'O LORD of hosts, if you will indeed look on the affliction of your servant and remember me and not forget your servant, but will give to your servant a son, then I will give him to the Lord all the days of his life, and no razor shall touch his head" (1 Sam. 1:10-11, *ESV*). Hannah began praying in such grief that the priest, Eli, thought she was drunk! She responded to him by saying that she was a troubled woman pouring out her soul to the Lord. In verse 16, Hannah cries, "Do not regard your servant as a worthless woman, for all along I have been speaking out of my great anxiety and vexation."

What do we find out in this remarkable passage about Hannah? She was as real as real could be! I find it fascinating that she did not try to hide her true feelings and that her utmost request to God was for a child. After she prayed and poured out her soul in desperate authenticity before God, she was no longer sad; and she even began to eat again. Verse 19 declares that she worshiped before the Lord the next morning before returning home.

So, what is so fascinating about Hannah in this passage? Her faith was manifested *after* her authenticity. After pouring out her soul to God, she worshiped. Hannah had no idea at this point that she was going to have a baby! Her worship (faith) came after she wept bitterly before the Lord. Hannah did not have on a mask. She was real. In verses 19 and 20, we discover that God blessed Hannah and she gave birth to a son.

We must be real with God for Him to be real with us! The Lord already knows all about us, but He is waiting for us to be real with Him. Remember, He desires truth. He already knows the truth about you and about me. Yet, He never forces Himself on us. He has given us a choice to respond to Him out of authenticity or to reject Him out of fabrication. Jesus said, "I stand at the door and knock. If anyone hears my voice and opens the door, I will come in to him and eat with him, and he with me" (Rev. 3:20, *ESV*). Have you opened the door of your heart to the one who desires to reveal Himself to you?

Are you ready to know who you are, defined by God instead of by your past experiences? Are you tired of wearing a mask? It is possible for you to know your true identity and live life in reality.

The first step in living life without a mask is to admit that you want to be real, honest, truthful and genuine with yourself and with God. Are you ready to discover more fully who you are and why you were created? You can start with this prayer.

Dear God,
I must admit I have worn a mask for a very
long time. I struggle with knowing who I am and
who You created me to be. Fear of not being loved and
accepted torments me. I have difficulty loving myself at times
and accepting who You have created me to be. I need You in my
life. I don't want to live life with a mask, but I desire to be real
with You. Please help me to be truthful. I am admitting
my desire to live life in reality. Please enable
me to more fully experience Your love and understand
who I am and the purpose You have for me.
In Your name I pray, amen.

YOUR PRAYER

_____

_____

_____

_____

_____

_____

_____

_____

_____

WHAT DO YOU THINK?

What do you remember wanting to be when you were a little girl?

_____

_____

_____

Why do you think you wanted to be what you listed above?

_____

_____

_____

In what ways have you struggled with trying to figure out who you are?

_____

_____

_____

Why do you think reality is something we long to escape from?

_____
_____
_____
_____
_____

What do you think it means to be real?

_____
_____
_____
_____
_____

What is the first step in living life without a mask?

_____
_____
_____
_____
_____

Are you ready to be real with yourself and God?

_____
_____
_____
_____
_____

List some of the struggles and issues you need God's help with but so often try to run away from.

_____
_____
_____
_____
_____

Unchanging Truths to Read and Treasure

PSALM 51:6
JOHN 8:32

Notes
1. Margery Williams, *The Velveteen Rabbit* (Franklin, TN: The Dalmatian Press, 1999).
2. "Real," The Free Dictionary, http://www.thefreedictionary.com/real.
3. "Real," Encarta Dictionary. Encarta® World English Dictionary (North American Edition), Microsoft Corporation, 2009.

CHAPTER TWO

Who Am I?

For You formed my inward parts; You covered me in my mother's womb.
I will praise You, for I am fearfully and wonderfully made; marvelous are
Your works, and that my soul knows very well.
PSALM 139:13-14

Therefore, if anyone is in Christ, he is a new creation; old things have
passed away; behold, all things have become new.
2 CORINTHIANS 5:17

I was in the seventh grade when I realized I had an eating disorder. Unbeknownst to me, my mother had opened the door of the bathroom and saw my revealing backbone as I stepped out of the shower. She was so startled and alarmed that it brought her to the point of tears. She quietly closed the bathroom door so that I would remain unaware of her presence. Later, she shared with me that I looked like a skeleton and it had literally taken her breath away. She was shocked at the sight of my malnourished body and didn't know what to do or where to turn for help and counsel.

I had never heard of anorexia nervosa or any other eating disorder until my mother approached me with the terminology. All I knew was that something crazy was going on inside of me.

As time passed, I became a very insecure teenage girl and felt like I was on a continual cycle to measure up to some standard I didn't exactly know how to define and didn't know how to reach. I do remember being excessively influenced by the words and thoughts of others. When anyone made an observation about me, whether it was positive or negative, I didn't know how to receive it. Their words often dictated what I believed about myself or believed I should be. In essence, my identity was found in the opinions and judgments of others.

I remember an older woman in our church who came up to me and told me how glad she was that her preacher's daughter was skinny. Was she trying to give me a compliment? To this woman's benefit, I know she had no idea of the inner struggle with which I was battling on a daily basis; but her words definitely did not help my anorexic mentality. I left her presence thinking to myself that I must never gain weight, because that is what everyone expects—the pastor's daughter should be skinny.

I have always had a petite frame and never struggled with my weight as a little girl. I loved to eat. I enjoyed food and didn't think twice about it. So I honestly don't know how an eating disorder took me captive so quickly or how it all began. Perhaps you can relate with the previous sentence. Or, if you haven't had this struggle, possibly you know someone who is struggling with an eating disorder but you don't know how to offer support or understanding.

What I know for sure about my struggle is that I constantly felt out of control. Maybe it's because I didn't have a good understanding of all the changes going on inside of me during preadolescence, or the changes I saw in my friends. I stopped eating because it was the only thing I felt I could control. My eating disorder didn't begin as a body image problem; it began with an uncertainty and confusion as to who I was created to be; it began with my lack of understanding of my identity. I didn't know the answer to the question: *Who am I?*

As the eating disorder advanced, it later developed into a body image problem. I would look in the mirror and always see myself as lacking. I was never pretty enough; never skinny enough; never tall enough; never good enough. I never thought I measured up. When we don't know how to answer the question, *Who am I?* we often turn to behaviors that bring us some sense of being in control—anorexia, bulimia, overeating, cutting, substance abuse, premarital sex . . . and the list goes on.

I remember one evening when the Miss America pageant was on TV. I loved watching the beautiful young women, in their long dresses, walk with confidence and poise in front of the audience. I vividly remember dressing up, putting on makeup and curling my hair before I felt like I could sit down and watch the show. Why? I didn't measure up. I wanted so desperately to fit into the mold of what I thought personified true beauty and confidence. I wanted acceptance and security.

I became very particular about food. In fact, I became so wrapped up in bondage to control of what I ate that all I thought about was calorie intake and food on a minute-by-minute basis. I could tell you what I had eaten up to two weeks prior, every single day. It obsessed me. It entangled me. It seemed as if I was in a bottomless pit of bondage and didn't know how to get out. The more I endeavored to take control, the more out of control I became.

The day after my mother saw me in the bathroom, she dropped me off at school without saying a word and went to the public library to find every book she could get her hands on about eating disorders. After hours of reading, she was convinced that I had all the symptoms of anorexia nervosa. When she got home, she threw herself on my little day bed and cried out to God, asking Him for help.

Although I had a true relationship with Jesus Christ, I didn't have a clear understanding of my identity in Christ and how God created me as His beautiful creation.

My mother began searching the Scriptures, God's Holy Word, in order to share the truth with me. I did believe the Bible was true, and my mother knew she could share the Scriptures with me and I would have a better understanding of my identity. She prayed for the Lord to show her how to approach me and what to say, and He did just that.

When my mother talked with me after school, I responded in a very broken manner. As she began to convey to me how special I was to her, to my father and to God, I remember feeling so scared and insecure. I wanted so desperately to get better, but I didn't know how to get there. After my mother helped me understand what I was going through, I admitted that I was struggling and that I wanted to get better.

I wish I could tell you that I was instantly healed, but it took time. Through it all, however, I began to embrace who my Creator designed me to be.

My battle with anorexia lasted four years. The last two years were mostly spent in recovery. I would have good days and bad days. At my worst, I weighed 62 pounds in the eighth grade, with a goal of weighing 55 pounds. When my hair started to come out, it really freaked me out big-time, and something went off in my head that made me realize I was sick and had a big problem.

I began to read God's Word daily; and the more I saturated myself with truth, the healthier I became. It felt like I was in combat every day. I memorized Matthew 6:25-34, which my mother

shared with me on the day she saw that I was anorexic, and it became a touchstone for me:

> Therefore I say to you, do not worry about your life, what
> you will eat or what you will drink; nor about your body,
> what you will put on. Is not life more than food and the
> body more than clothing? Look at the birds of the air, for
> they neither sow nor reap nor gather into barns; yet your
> heavenly Father feeds them. Are you not of more value than
> they? Which of you by worrying can add one cubit to his
> stature? So why do you worry about clothing? Consider the
> lilies of the field, how they grow: they neither toil nor spin;
> and yet I say to you that even Solomon in all his glory was
> not arrayed like one of these. Now if God so clothes the
> grass of the field, which today is, and tomorrow is thrown
> into the oven, will He not much more clothe you, O you of
> little faith? "Therefore do not worry, saying, 'What shall we
> eat?' or 'What shall we drink?' or 'What shall we wear?' For
> after all these things the Gentiles seek. For your heavenly
> Father knows that you need all these things. But seek first
> the kingdom of God and His righteousness, and all these
> things shall be added to you. Therefore do not worry about
> tomorrow, for tomorrow will worry about its own things.
> Sufficient for the day is its own trouble.

I realize this passage isn't referring specifically to the anorexic
or her struggle with food. The people in this passage were actually
concerned about where they were going to find food and clothing
for survival. However, this entire passage has everything to do with
worry and anxiety—attitudes that consumed my life in connection
with food. Although I memorized this passage, I often read it from
my Bible—sometimes more than 20 times a day, for four years. The
Word of God became my medicine. I had to ingest it for survival.

In high school, the Word of God became a constant necessity.
Whenever a lie came into my mind, such as, "You're not good

enough" or "You're not pretty enough," I would begin to read the Word of God. I wanted to memorize the Word in case I found myself without access to it. Constant reinforcement from God's Word helped me more than anything else.

The Word of God is so powerful because it consists of 100 percent truth. The apostle Paul tells us that God cannot lie (see Titus 1:2). It is impossible for God to lie! Satan is the polar opposite of God, and Scripture calls him the father of lies (see John 8:44). I had believed so many lies; but I learned that truth always overcomes lies. I might have continued to struggle with my issues instead of looking at the root of the problem—understanding who I am in Christ—if I had not saturated myself with the truth of God's Word. Here is a prime example of countering Satan's lies with the truth:

> Beloved, do not believe every spirit, but test the spirits, whether they are of God; because many false prophets have gone out into the world. By this you know the Spirit of God: Every spirit that confesses that Jesus Christ has come in the flesh is of God, and every spirit that does not confess that Jesus Christ has come in the flesh is not of God. And this is the spirit of the Antichrist, which you have heard was coming, and is now already in the world. *You are of God, little children, and have overcome them, because he who is in you is greater than he who is in the world.* They are of the world. Therefore they speak as of the world, and the world hears them. We are of God. He who knows God hears us; he who is not of God does not hear us. By this we know the spirit of truth and the spirit of error (1 John 4:1-6, emphasis added).

Satan desperately desires that we believe in him rather than in God. He desires that we live our entire lives believing in lies instead of the truth that will set us free (see John 8:32).

Before I embraced a biblical view of my Creator God and started believing that He really did love me, my life consisted of fear. These kinds of questions continually floated in and out of my consciousness: *Does God really love me? Does He truly accept me, no matter what? Was I created intentionally, or am I a mistake or an accident?*

I found release from my fears in the truth of such words as these found in 1 John 4:18-19: "There is no fear in love; but perfect love casts our fear, because fear involves torment. But he who fears has not been made perfect in love. We love Him because He first loved us." Words that are better than any medicine!

Your Identity Unmasked

There is another passage of Scripture that helped me understand my identity, and I believe it will help you too. We can learn so much about who God is, how He created us and who we are as His beautiful creation, by reading and meditating on Psalm 139:

> O LORD, You have searched me and known me.
> You know my sitting down and my rising up;
>> You understand my thought afar off.
> You comprehend my path and my lying down,
>> And are acquainted with all my ways.
> For there is not a word on my tongue,
>> But behold, O LORD, You know it altogether.
> You have hedged me behind and before,
>> And laid Your hand upon me.
> Such knowledge is too wonderful for me;
>> It is high, I cannot attain it.
>
> Where can I go from Your Spirit?
>> Or where can I flee from Your presence?
> If I ascend into heaven, You are there;
>> If I make my bed in hell, behold, You are there.
> If I take the wings of the morning,
>> And dwell in the uttermost parts of the sea,
> Even there Your hand shall lead me,
>> And Your right hand shall hold me.

If I say, "Surely the darkness shall fall on me,"
    Even the night shall be light about me;
Indeed, the darkness shall not hide from You,
    But the night shines as the day;
    The darkness and the light are both alike to You.

For You formed my inward parts;
    You covered me in my mother's womb.
I will praise You, for I am fearfully and wonderfully made;
    Marvelous are Your works,
    And that my soul knows very well.
My frame was not hidden from You,
    When I was made in secret,
    And skillfully wrought in the lowest parts of the earth.
Your eyes saw my substance, being yet unformed.
    And in Your book they all were written,
    The days fashioned for me,
    When as yet there were none of them.

How precious also are Your thoughts to me, O God!
    How great is the sum of them!
If I should count them, they would be more in number
    than the sand;
    When I awake, I am still with You.

Oh, that You would slay the wicked, O God!
    Depart from me, therefore, you bloodthirsty men.
For they speak against You wickedly;
    Your enemies take Your name in vain.
Do I not hate them, O LORD, who hate You?
    And do I not loathe those who rise up against You?
I hate them with perfect hatred; I count them my enemies.

Search me, O God, and know my heart;
    Try me, and know my anxieties;
And see if there is any wicked way in me,
    And lead me in the way everlasting.

I've often read this passage, but sometimes its meaning doesn't completely sink in because there is such a depth and richness to it. This encouraging passage assures us that we have been "fearfully and wonderfully made." Still, there are times when I don't see myself as lovable or beautiful. I don't feel like I measure up. Do you ever struggle with thoughts like that? Those are the times when you must go to His Word to restore your understanding of who God says you are.

Let's take a closer look at this psalm to get a better understanding of all that is going on here. First of all, David is actually having a conversation with God. As you read the first verse and apply it, "O Lord, You have searched me and known me," your first thought may not necessarily be a comfortable one.

I remember this as if it happened yesterday: the first time I got pulled over by a policeman. I was 16 years old, and on my way to school. I had just begun to drive by myself. Seeing the blue blinking lights in my rearview mirror created a rush of panic all through me. I drove into a grocery store parking lot and sat there in my light blue Dodge Daytona sports car as the intimidating police officer walked up to my car window. I knew I wasn't speeding, and I couldn't imagine what I had done wrong; yet I was extremely nervous. I didn't say a word.

The officer asked me for my license, registration and then began to ask me a set of questions. I felt like a horrible person although the reason he pulled me over was because my rear brake light was out. The office gave me a warning, and I left there trembling and crying. The worst thing was that in the middle of it all, I felt out of control. I didn't know what was going on or what I had done. Although I had been pulled over for a rear brake light, this policeman asked me question after question. I learned later that by law he had to ask specific questions to properly search a civilian.

The word "search" used in Psalm 139:1 means "to turn upside down" or "to ransack." Just as I felt out of control when I didn't know what I was being pulled over for by the police officer, there are times in life when your world is turned upside down and you feel out of control. At times the Lord purposefully allows your life to be turned upside down to get your attention. Now do you like this verse? Not particularly, right? The feeling of being turned upside down is not that thrilling to me either, even on a roller-coaster ride. However, this term also reveals the detail in which the Lord knows everything about us. He knows the good, the bad, the pretty and the ugly. He searches our hearts and knows our frame. This leads us to Unchanging Truth #1: *God has perfect knowledge of you.*

UNCHANGING TRUTH #1:
God Has Perfect Knowledge of You

In the second part of verse 1, David is saying to God, not only have You turned my life upside down, but *You also know me.* If you are saying to yourself right now, *Okay . . . what's the big deal? God knows me. That's great,* then perhaps you are more comfortable with yourself than I am with me. This verse makes me feel embarrassed, because I know the real me at my worst. The real me is insecure. The real me desires sin. The real me makes wrong decisions. The real me is prideful. The real me is jealous. The real me is confused. The real me feels forgotten. The real me doesn't desire God. The real me needs help.

Be honest; do you really feel comfortable with someone knowing the real you—the "you" apart from God in your life? Yet, God knows everything about you. And still He loves you. Remember 1 John 4:19? "We love Him because He first loved us." God loves you. Who you are is found in who He is. The first unchanging truth to discover about God in this enlightening passage is that *He has a perfect knowledge of you.* Get past the embarrassment and you will find true comfort in this.

So far, we have discovered that God turns our lives upside down at times to get our attention, and He knows the part of us that we don't want anyone to ever know. Talk about a personal God! He is more personal than you could ever imagine.

Let's look at Psalm 139:2. I'll bet you hope this is going to get more comfortable, right? This verse reads, "You know my sitting down and my rising up." What do you think sitting down and rising up has to do with God's knowledge of you? Have you ever counted the number of times you have literally sat down and gotten up in one day? So what is the meaning here? Sitting down and rising up represent everyday occurrences. God knows you to the extent that He is aware of the simple, everyday tasks you do. That's some knowledge!

The second part of verse 2 gets even more personal: "You understand my thought afar off." Are you kidding me? I don't even understand my thoughts. Have you ever wondered what it would be like if your thoughts were recorded for everyone to hear? Now that's a scary thought!

- *Oh my, look at what she's wearing . . . I wouldn't be caught dead in that!*
- *Look at him. Now he looks good.*
- *This professor is so boring.*
- *I wish I could just smack him.*
- *Who does she think she is talking to my boyfriend like that?*
- *Should I eat that donut?*
- *I am so fat, why would anyone ever like me.*
- *Why is he smiling at me? Is he smiling at me?*

We may also think a lot of choice words toward people we don't like or people who may get on our nerves; or we might even say these words to ourselves about ourselves. Words said or not said, God hears them all, and He knows our thoughts.

In verse 3, David is communicating with God in relation to life's direction. "You comprehend my path and my lying down. You are acquainted with all my ways." Doesn't this verse sometimes make you want to run and hide? But, wait, He knows that too. If you are feeling good about what you are reading so far, then I don't think you are getting the actual content of this verse. Think about your ways. Are they *all* good? Mine are not.

In verse 4, David says that there is not a word on his tongue that the Lord doesn't already know. Oh no, now we are all in trouble! He really does know every single detail about our lives. Verse 5 says, "You have hedged me behind and before, and laid Your hand upon me." At this point in the passage, as David is saying that God knows everything about him, I would think God would say, "Okay, forget you. You're a hopeless case." David's response begins in verse 6, when he conveys his feeling that God knowing everything about him is extremely difficult to grasp.

After understanding the reality that God has a perfect knowledge of him, David says, in verse 7, "Where can I go from Your Spirit? Or where can I flee from Your presence?" David is saying, because You know the real me, how can I get away from You? Where can I go to hide to get away from this truth? We often feel like this when we are faced with a true picture of who we are and the help we need, which leads us to Unchanging Truth #2: *God is always present*.

UNCHANGING TRUTH #2:
God Is Always Present

God is always there. He always has been and He always will be. He is omnipresent.

When I was in junior high, I remember calling my father's secretary and asking her to come and pick me up from school because I was sick. I couldn't get in touch with my parents, so I had decided to call the secretary. Well, the truth of the matter was that I wasn't sick at all. I just wanted to go home, so I lied.

Usually a lie like this can be easy to cover up, right? Well, needless to say, it didn't go in my favor on this bright spring day in April. I remember hearing my parents come home, and I ran to the back bedroom and jumped as fast as I could under the blankets.

They could tell that I really wasn't sick, even though I tried to pretend. I thought it would be the end of the story after I confessed to them; but my father made me go over to the church office, confess to his secretary what I had done and ask her forgiveness for lying. Talk about humiliating! That was the last place I wanted to go. I wanted to stay in my room, and I never wanted her to know the truth. I remember not wanting to face her and yet being shocked that she forgave me when I admitted the truth.

We all prefer hiding from the truth at times. David was asking God how He could get away from Him, while at the same time being faced with the reality that it was utterly impossible to ever escape God's presence when he belonged to Him. Did you get that? Once you come into a relationship with God, it is impossible to stop being His daughter. Once you are His, you will always be His, regardless of anything you do. Remember 1 John 4:4? This is a powerful verse, but we must not overlook what it says: "He who is *in you* is greater than he who is in the world." In order to know who you are and be free from bondage, God must take residence in your life. Is God *in you*? This is the first step to embracing your true identity. You must first know who your Creator is before you will ever know who you are. You must know that He is in you.

After David realizes that he cannot hide from God, he is reminded of the unique creation of God that he is. God created each one of us differently for His purposes. Verses 13-14 tell us, "For You [God] formed my inward parts; You covered me in my mother's womb. I will praise You for I am fearfully and wonderfully made; marvelous are Your works, and that my soul knows very well." This beautiful declaration leads us to Unchanging Truth #3: *God is your designer who uniquely and purposefully created you.*

Unchanging Truth #3:
God Uniquely and Purposefully Created You

There is a major difference in having head knowledge concerning what God says about you and believing it in your heart. So often I don't like the way God made me. I get up in the morning, crawl out of the bed, look in the mirror and say to myself, *Ah! Who is that?* It has been in those times of insecurity, especially when I struggled as an anorexic, that I was reminded that God created me the way He did, and I am loved unconditionally by Him, no matter what I may look like or feel like inside. I am no accident; you are no accident.

Charles Spurgeon was a gifted pastor who was named the "Prince of Pastors" in the 1850s. He was married to a God-fearing woman named Susannah. He often reflected on what it meant to be "fearfully and wonderfully made." Here is a small portion of what he wrote about Psalm 139:

> For I am fearfully and wonderfully made. Who can gaze even upon a model of our anatomy without wonder and awe? Who could dissect a portion of the human frame without marveling at its delicacy, and trembling at its frailty? The Psalmist had scarcely peered within the veil which hides the nerves, sinews, and blood vessels from common inspection; the science of anatomy was quite unknown to him; and yet he had seen enough to arouse his admiration of the work and his reverence for the Worker. Marvelous are thy works. These parts of my frame are all thy works; and though they be home works, close under my own eye, yet are they wonderful to the last degree. They are works within my own self, yet are they beyond my understanding, and appear to me as so many miracles of skill and power. We need not go to the ends of the earth for marvels, nor even across our own threshold; they abound in our own bodies.[1]

To be fearfully and wonderfully made means that God created you uniquely and purposefully. You are unlike anyone else. He has created you the way you are, even what you look like. He has designed you for a reason and has a destiny for your life. You are His handiwork, and He is your Artist. Regardless of what you may think or feel, you are God's masterpiece!

Embrace God's Design for You

After reading such an amazing passage of truth from Psalm 139, we can accept the fact that God desires us just the way we are.

Thus, we have no reason to hide or pretend. Our Creator is the one who desires to give us our identity unmasked. Once we embrace His design for our lives, then we have no reason to try to be someone we are not. We were never created to be anyone other than who we are, filled with Jesus. When we accept the truth that God is the one making us into what He has designed us to be, we understand that the journey toward discovering our identity is dependent on simply a surrendered heart yielded to our Creator. He created us the way we are, for a reason. We are no accident or mistake.

As David expresses the truth that he has been created uniquely, he goes on to say, "My frame was not hidden from You, when I was made in secret, and skillfully wrought in the lowest parts of the earth. Your eyes saw my substance, being yet unformed. And in Your book, they all were written, the days fashioned for me, when as yet there were none of them" (Ps. 139:15-16). Before anyone else knew that David was going to exist, God knew. Nothing that God creates is an accident. Each one of us was sovereignly planned in the heart of God before anyone else knew we were going to exist. Regardless of the circumstances surrounding your birth, God specifically chose you to be born. I repeat, you are no mistake or accident.

In verses 17-18, David conveys how precious are the thoughts that God thinks toward him; and if he would be able to count them, they would be more in number than the sand. I don't know what you are thinking about that, but I think that is a lot of thoughts about us! That leads us to Unchanging Truth #4: *God loves you and cares for you. You are always on His mind.*

UNCHANGING TRUTH #4:
You Are Always on God's Mind

Have you ever cared about someone to the point that you literally couldn't get him or her off your mind, even though you tried your hardest to forget? It's like you think about this person constantly, and there would never be a way to count how many times a day this person is in your thoughts. This happens especially when you

Monica Rose Brennan · www.regalbooks.com

meet the man of your dreams . . . or the man you think is the man of your dreams. You think about him constantly and have every single word in your mind that he said the day before . . . and you hope and pray that he is thinking about you constantly too.

God thinks about us constantly, but on a much grander scale than we could ever comprehend. He loves us so much. In Psalm 68:5, David tells us that God is a father of the fatherless. Even when we feel like others may have abandoned us or don't care for us, God says that He will be our Father.

I was a freshman in college the first time I visited a homeless shelter. I began working with children in that shelter every Sunday night. A group of us would show up at 5:00 PM and serve food to all who were there; then I would go back into an area just for the children and feed them before teaching them songs and sharing a Bible story with them.

One day, I walked into the room and saw a precious little blonde-headed girl who was probably not more than four years old. She gave me a big smile, although she could hardly look up because of the pain she was experiencing in her neck. There was a large bruise on the right side of her neck, and she was not able to even turn her head. There were signs of malnutrition and severe physical abuse all over her little body. Her clothes were filthy and smelly. My heart went out to this little girl, and I had to push every emotion back to stop myself from crying.

As we gathered on the floor for our Bible story time, she approached me, asking me if she could sit in my lap on the floor. Of course I said yes. She leaned her little body up against me during the story. At one point, something very remarkable happened. She took both of my hands and placed them tightly around her waist. Every few seconds she would make a gasping sound because her body was so tender from her physical injuries, but she wouldn't let me remove my arms from around her waist. She desired love more than the feeling of being without pain.

I often think about that little girl in the homeless shelter. I think about the fact that we all desire so desperately to be loved and to be secure. I think about the fact that when everybody else abandons us, God loves us and cares for us. I was able to whisper into this four-year-old girl's ear, "Jesus loves you so much." Every Sunday I would return and tell her the same thing: "Jesus loves you so much." In Psalm 27:10, David says, "For my father and my mother have forsaken me, but the LORD will take me in" (*ESV*).

Who Am I?

"Who am I?" can only be answered by embracing the truths of who God is. To do that, let's recap the four Unchanging Truths found in Psalm 139:

- Unchanging Truth #1: God has perfect knowledge of you.
- Unchanging Truth #2: God is omnipresent—He is always with you.
- Unchanging Truth #3: God is your designer who uniquely and purposefully created you. You are no accident.
- Unchanging Truth #4: God loves you and cares for you. You are always on His mind.

The truths are there for you to read and meditate on in Psalm 139. God is your Designer. He has a plan for everything, regardless of what happens in your life. He is God and you are not. He is the Creator of you; you are not the designer of Him. Although God has perfect knowledge of you, He still loves you and has a plan for your life.

We All Need a Savior

If we are truly honest with ourselves, the "real" person within the deepest part of our souls is often:

• hopeless	• desperate	• prideful
• fearful	• frustrated	• searching
• needy	• selfish	• jealous

- depressed   · sinful   · lost
- anxious

We all need something real. We all need hope. We all need security. We all need fulfillment, peace and direction. We need understanding. We need truth. We need God. We are in need of a true knowledge of who God is. Then we can know who we are and what difference that makes. Most of all, we need Jesus; it is only in Him that we have life, for He is the life (see John 14:6).

Regardless of background, experiences, age, ethnic group or religion, we all need a Savior. We are in need of His grace, love, restoration and mercy. Because some people choose not to respond to the Savior, it is possible for them to live all of their life without knowing who they are or why they are here. We must know God to know ourselves.

The Bible teaches that in order to really know God, we must have a relationship with His Son, Jesus Christ. *Do you know Him?* By inviting Him into your life, you are declaring your belief in Jesus. By asking Him to forgive you of all of your sins, you are asking Him to make you into a new creation and give you an identity unmasked. Paul wrote in 2 Corinthians 5:17, "Therefore, if anyone is in Christ, he is a new creation; old things have passed away; behold, all things have become new."

To become a new creation in Christ and discover your identity, you must ask Jesus Christ into your life. When you make this decision, you are saying yes to His will and plan for your life. The Bible calls this salvation. God is your Creator and Designer, and He knows what is best for you.

I encourage you to get into the Word of God, because it is truth. It is only when you saturate yourself with truth that you can overcome the lies that keep you weighed down and held captive.

It's a Daily Journey

I am confident that the Word of God healed me from my eating disorder. During my struggle with anorexia and my search to answer the question "Who am I?" my parents were also a strong support to me. My mother would often have to literally place food in front of me, and say, "Eat this or you will die." With the Lord's help, with my parents' support, and with a strong, personal desire to receive help and be healed, I recovered completely from this eating disorder, and now it is simply a distant memory.

I remember the first day when I did not continually think about food. Then a week passed without my thoughts obsessively returning to food . . . then two weeks . . . then a month. It was such a relief! My mother and I actually celebrated the day I started my menstrual cycle. I was almost a junior in high school and still had not begun menstruating. We actually prayed about this because we felt that my first period would be evidence that I really was getting better.

Throughout the four years of my anorexia, I began to see and understand better who I was and how God saw me. Even though I didn't feel like I measured up, God said that He had made me for a purpose, and He had made me unique and special. I found acceptance in Christ, although at times I didn't accept myself. *I realized for the first time that my identity was found in Christ, not in how I looked or felt that I measured up.*

I still have days when I feel lost, forgotten, unlovely, guilty, confused, lonely, insecure. Whew! However, I have come to realize that discovering who I am is a journey, and it is not based on how I feel. God is still at work in me. I don't have it all figured out, but I do know the one who does. I've also realized that it is impossible to embark on this journey *apart from Christ*.

Gaining an understanding of who you are in Christ is not a one-time decision, but a determination you make every day. I know that every day, I must be reminded that He is the one who defines me, because He is the one who created me. He is the one who gives me an identity unmasked. He is the one who can tell me who I am because He knows me better than I know myself.

Will you walk this daily journey with me—the journey of discovering who you were created to be and how to embrace the one who so longs to give you an identity and a purpose? If you are ready to go deeper, let's begin with a prayer.

Dear God,
Thank You for being a God who cannot lie. Help me to
believe in You and in Your unchanging truths. Thank You for
creating me for a reason and a purpose. Forgive me for
placing my identity in the opinions of others. May I focus
only on who You say I am—Your beautiful creation.
Enable me to go deeper in my journey with You.
In Your name I pray, amen.

YOUR PRAYER

_____
_____
_____
_____
_____
_____
_____
_____
_____
_____
_____
_____
_____
_____
_____

WHAT DO YOU THINK?

Describe a time when you felt like you didn't measure up.

_____

_____

_____

_____

What do you struggle with in your attempt to discover your identity and find acceptance from others?

_____

_____

_____

_____

Have you ever succumbed to an eating disorder or another type of behavior—cutting, substance abuse, premarital sex—so that you can feel like you are "taking control"? If so, describe your battle.

_____

_____

_____

_____

List the two main problems the people were wrestling with in Matthew 6:25-34 that can help you realize how valuable you are to God.

_____

_____

_____

_____

Describe the two spirits discussed in John 4:1-4. Which spirit can
be trusted? Why? Which spirit are you listening to?

_____

_____

_____

_____

What are the four unchanging truths found in Psalm 139 and discussed in this chapter? How does this knowledge change your understanding of who God is and who you were created to be?

_____

_____

_____

_____

What is the first step toward unmasking your true identity? Have
you taken this step?

_____

_____

_____

Unchanging Truths to Read and Treasure

PSALM 139
MATTHEW 6:25-34
2 CORINTHIANS 5:17

Note

1. Charles H. Spurgeon, "Commentary on Psalm 139:14," *The Treasury of David.* http://
   bible.crosswalk.com/Commentaries/TreasuryofDavid/tod.cgi?book=ps&chap
   ter=139&verse=014.

CHAPTER THREE

Is Perception Reality?

"To whom then will you liken Me,
or to whom shall I be equal?" says the Holy One.
ISAIAH 40:25

Now faith is the substance of things hoped for, the evidence of things not
seen. For by it the elders obtained a good testimony. By faith we under-
stand that the worlds were framed by the word of God, so that the things
which are seen were not made of things which are visible. . . . Without faith
it is impossible to please Him, for he who comes to God must believe that
He is, and that He is a rewarder of those who diligently seek Him.
HEBREWS 11:1-3,6

H ave you ever questioned God? Have you ever blamed God for things that happen outside of your control? Have you ever blamed Him when things didn't make sense? Have you ever asked yourself, *Who is this God who says He knows me better than I know myself? Who is this God who seeks to show me who I am?*

When we think of who God is, we must understand that we already have some thoughts about who we *think* He is, regardless of whether they are right or wrong. Who God truly is and how we perceive God can be two different things. Perception is not always reality.

When I was anorexic, I thought I looked overweight when I looked in the mirror. My perception of myself was distorted. I weighed only 62 pounds, but I saw myself as fat. In reality, I was very skinny. I thought of myself as healthy. In reality, I was very sick. I was deceived in the way I viewed myself.

A Distorted View of God

Often we have our own personal views or opinions of who we think God is, based on our life experiences or what we want God to be like for us. For example, if we grow discouraged about something, we often blame God, regardless of whether or not we vocalize an actual belief in Him. A friend said to me, after church one Sunday, "I'm so angry with God! Why is He causing my friend to experience so much pain?" We often begin to dislike God if something bad happens, even though the Sunday before we were raising our hands to Him in a worship service or playing a praise song in the band.

We often seek to make God into someone He is not. We redefine God in our own minds and make Him what we want Him to be for us instead of allowing Him to stand alone in the truth of who He really is. Scripture tells us that there is no other like God: "'To whom then will you liken Me, or to whom shall I be equal?' says the Holy One" (Isa. 40:25).

Our experiences can turn into false perceptions if we allow our personal opinions about God to take center stage over the truth we find out about God in Scripture. Often our feelings toward God at any given moment can replace our faith in Him. Hebrews 11:6 tells us, "But without faith it is impossible to please Him, for he who comes to God must believe that He is, and that He is a rewarder of those who diligently seek Him." Faith is not a feeling; it is a surrender of our mindset to believe God regardless of any temptation, trial or test we may be facing.

We must come to grips with the reality of who God is and who we are in relation to Him. Easier said than done, right? As we attempt to discover who God is and who we were created to be, it is impossible to have a proper view of self apart from a proper view of God. These two are and always will be connected for an accurate understanding of self-identity.

A Distorted View of Self

Self is not something you can discover by seeking it out or by focusing completely on being a "better" person. *Self* is also not something you can discover by placing more attention on yourself. Rather, *self* is found only in a true knowledge and accurate understanding of who your Creator is, according to Scripture. In other words, it is impossible to discover the "be" (who you are) by seeking the "do" (your own efforts at identifying yourself). Yet, we often try to find our identity in the doing and not the being.

Our identity is only found in "being"—not in our own "being," but in understanding and knowing the "being" of Christ (who He is). Therefore, *for me to know who I am, I must first know who He is.* I can also conclude:

A false view of God = a false view of self

Most of us have a false view of God. Thus, we are literally incapable of seeing ourselves for who we were created to be. We base our thoughts and opinions about God solely on our personal experiences and traditions. Instead of digging deep into

God's truth and being completely changed and captured by the Scriptures, we tend to give greater weight to false truths found in magazines and movies. Are you with me here? Our belief system can get so mixed up when we are being molded by false messages of what it means to be a woman in the twenty-first century. We really need a true view of who God is to know who we were intentionally created to be.

One of the things I enjoy doing, especially in the wintertime, is going to a coffee shop and ordering a vanilla latte or a chai tea to drink, while reading Scripture or a really good devotional book. Just the other day, I was having coffee with a friend, a student of mine, who asked me if we could catch up on life. Upon the first sip of my delicious vanilla latte, my friend wasted no time informing me that she had decided to embrace the lesbian lifestyle. Although I was surprised at this news, I appreciated her authenticity about the entire situation and her openness. She went on to share with me that this was a decision she had made and she just wanted to be up front and real about it and wanted me to know.

I just sat there listening to her talk, justifying her decision "biblically." Countless times during our conversation, my dear friend reiterated the fact that she was a Christian who genuinely loved Jesus Christ. She had dated young men in the past but never felt fully accepted by them. She went on to say that "the Lord" had given her complete peace about this lifestyle. She began to show me several verses in Scripture pertaining to God's love.

After a couple hours of my friend sharing with me about her decision and justifying her behavior "based on Scripture," she then asked me what I thought. I was both honored and shocked that she asked my opinion on this subject. I just sat there for a few seconds and then responded, "I so appreciate your sharing with me, and I want you to know how much God loves you and how intentional He was in creating you. He created you as a female and has designed His order of creation to follow His plan for relationships. Scripture is clear that God's plan for marriage is between a man and a woman." I went on to say that God had a special plan for her life, regardless of her feelings, and that she would be blessed if she were to be obedient to God's design and order.

I asked my friend if I could share some Scripture with her as she had shared Scripture with me. My friend said yes as tears began to roll down her cheeks. We looked at verses concerning God's holiness as well as the way He designed the world in the beginning of time and created both male and female in His image and likeness. As I read to her from God's Word that He created both male and female, and what that meant, she didn't know exactly how to take it. It seemed as if she so desperately wanted to believe truth, but she had been listening to so many lies. She perceived herself to be someone she was never created to be because she had a wrong view and perception of God.

God is a God of love, but He is also a holy God who has a way for us to follow that will lead to life. My dear friend had made God into the image she wanted Him to be for her—a God of love, and only a God of love. By focusing on one single attribute of His being, she was able to justify her behavior. However, she was losing sight of the fact that God's image is not based on just one attribute, but on many attributes. Although God is a God of love, He is also a God who must be respected and revered. He is the one who created and designed the world and an order to the universe to be obeyed.

The Heart of Idolatry

When we read one verse of Scripture in isolation from others and fail to read a specific verse in context with the other surrounding verses, we place limits on our understanding in regard to what the whole of Scripture teaches. We lose the main point, the underlying principle and the basic meaning of the verse when we read one verse by itself. When we read Scripture like this, we take the meaning out of context. We make it say what it doesn't really mean.

It's fascinating to me how we would never think of picking up a short story or novel and read only one chapter and say we had completely understood the entire book from beginning to end.

Yet, at times, we handle God's Word like that. We are quick to read one verse out of context and conclude that it means something it was never meant to mean. We lose such rich, deep truth when we fail to read God's Word in its entirety and see God in His fullness by embracing all that He is, not just a part of who He is. No wonder we have difficulty perceiving a true view of God.

I think we often treat God's Word like a magazine. We pick it up randomly, flip through the different pages and read only what is in bold print, if that. A magazine is supposed to be read in that manner, but God's Word was never written to be read in a "flippant" manner. The truths contained in the Scriptures can transform the soul that is eager to find meaning and purpose to life. Because my friend simply saw God as only a God of love, it was easy for her to justify everything she was doing and say it was "okay" with God.

We are in great danger of coming up with an erroneous view of God and placing Him into the mold of self-satisfaction. Instead of allowing God to be who He is, we make Him into something or someone we want Him to be. We may say we worship "God," but the god or gods we worship have no attributes comparable to the true and living God. When we redefine who we want God to be or how we actually think He is, we are making a god in our own image. We begin worshiping a god we define, and not a God who defines us. This is idolatry.

Would you agree that there are times in which we all desire to sin and go against God's plan? There are times in which we all have redefined who God really is in order to justify our wrong thoughts and behavior. In those times, we seek to defend ourselves by saying that God's Word says something it really doesn't say, or saying we have "peace" from God even though His Word reveals something completely different. The problem with saying we have "peace" from God about something when His Word says something completely different is that God never, ever contradicts His Word. He never contradicts Himself! In fact, God and His Word are one.

John 1:1 declares, "In the beginning was the Word, and the Word was with God, and the Word was God." Remember, God doesn't lie. He doesn't say one thing in His Word and declare something completely opposite in our hearts. Hebrews 6:18 says that "it is impossible for God to lie." Indeed we are actually called "liars" if we say that Jesus Christ lives in us while we live in a way that is totally opposite to God's design for our lives. Here is what Scripture tells us:

> If we say we have fellowship with Him while we walk in darkness, we lie and do not practice the truth (1 John 1:6, *ESV*).

> Whoever says, "I know Him" but does not keep His commandments is a liar, and the truth is not in him, but whoever keeps His word, in him truly the love of God is perfected (1 John 2:4-5, *ESV*).

God Is Who He Says He Is

I often meet "Christian" young women who say they love Jesus with all their heart and want to make a difference in the world. Yet, they will choose to go out with a guy who is not a Christian. "But, Monica, I have so many feelings for this guy, and I have a peace that I am to date him. I know he isn't a Christian, but I can change him." Now, what is wrong with that mentality? Remember, God cannot contradict His Word; He is who He says He is. He would not give you a peace about something that His Word clearly teaches against. I assure you, you may have "peace," but it definitely is not from God. It is from the deceiver who wants you to have a misconstrued view of who God is and how God speaks.

The Lord doesn't want to make your life miserable, but His way is best. He has left us an amazing and truthful instructional manual to follow—the Bible—and it helps us know who He is. He desires that you live life to the fullest; but this is only possible if you have a true perception of Him!

Jesus reminds us of how different His motives are from Satan's deceiving ways, in John 10:10: "The thief does not come except to steal, and to kill, and to destroy. I have come that they may have life, and that they may have it more abundantly." His commandments are not given to keep us from the best, but to give us the best! At the same time, if we are walking in the truth of who God is, we will want to keep His commandments.

All throughout the psalms, the psalmist David expresses his love for God's commandments. In Psalm 119:47, he wrote, "For I find delight in your commandments, which I love" (*ESV*). Indeed, this is the true test to see if we have a pure relationship with the Lord Jesus. First John 5:2-3 declares, "By this we know that we love the children of God, when we love God and keep His commandments. For this is the love of God, that we keep His commandments. And His commandments are not burdensome."

On that cold winter day in the coffee shop, I shared with my friend that by following God's direction for our lives, we are choosing to live in a way that is holy—a way that pleases Him. Holy means *separate*. We are to be separate from the world.

So what does God's Word teach us about dating or marrying an unbeliever? The Scriptures show us that we are not to be in a relationship with a nonbeliever. Paul wrote in 2 Corinthians 6:14-16, "Do not be unequally yoked together with unbelievers. For what fellowship has righteousness with lawlessness? And what communion has light with darkness? And what accord has Christ with Belial? Or what part has a believer with an unbeliever? And what agreement has the temple of God with idols? For you are the temple of the living God."

The point we must ponder, and remember, is that God cannot contradict His Word. God and His Word are one; and what He says is always true.

Get Your Worldview from Scripture

Often we perceive God to be someone He is not because we do not have a true understanding of who He is from the Scriptures. We walk around with an *idea* of what we think God may or may not be, most of the time based solely on our opinion about a certain issue rather than the authority of Scripture.

Often, our perception of who we think God is and who He really is do not match, like my friend saying that God is love so that He wouldn't mind her being in a relationship that went against His design. When we make God into someone He is not, we are making it impossible for us to discover who we are. It is impossible for us to know who we are apart from who He is. A true view of God yields a true view of self.

Often we possess no fear of God (no appropriate reverence for who He is) because we have no clue about who He really is. To truly know God as a loving Father and also as the Holy One is to fear Him. Fear is not referring to a scary type of fear, but rather a fear in terms of reverence and worship. Succinctly put: He is God, and we are not.

A. W. Tozer, in his classic book *The Knowledge of the Holy*, wrote, "When men no longer fear God, they transgress His laws without hesitation. The fear of consequences is no deterrent when the fear of God is gone."[1] When we fail to see God as He is, we fall into deception, and our flesh responds to things that we once were able to stand against. Our identity is always placed in jeopardy when we fail to see God for who He really is. The apostle Paul declared, in 2 Corinthians 7:1, "Since we have these promises, beloved, let us cleanse ourselves from every defilement of body and spirit, bringing holiness to completion in the fear of God" (*ESV*).

If you wanted to continue to live in a sinful lifestyle but talked yourself into believing you were not doing anything wrong or sinful, you would be placing all your belief system on the love of God and forget about the fact that He is also a holy God. You would be making God in your own image. You would be seeking to redefine Him into the mold you want Him to be in and not what the Bible clearly teaches concerning who He is. If we are honest, we have all done this at one time or another.

It is crucial that we have a true view of who God is, because this is directly connected with the way we see ourselves. We were created in His image and likeness. I want to see a true picture of who God is.

I want to know the truth that can free me and give me an identity unmasked. Don't you?

My friend discovered that she didn't really know who she was or who God created her to be. Weeks after our conversation, she made the decision to embrace God's design for her life and repented from her sinful lifestyle. Her struggle was due to a false view of who God really is. God is love, but He is also holy. It is essential that we discover who God is before we can know who we are. A false perception of God will not do. We need a true understanding of the knowledge of God.

When We Question God's Character

So, who is He? *Who is God?* If someone came up to you and asked that question, how would you reply? If you were in a youth, college, or church gathering right now, and someone came up to you and asked you who God is, you probably would start naming various attributes, right? God is holy. God is just. God is truth. God is love. God is beautiful. God is sovereign. God is great. God is good. God is caring. God is merciful. God is long-suffering. God is kind. God is forgiving, and more. Or you might say something like, "Well . . . um . . . God is everything to me and He is the Creator of the world and, well . . . um, He's great." However, if you were honest with yourself in reference to how you really view God, your response might have a slightly different tone.

Let's be real for a moment about how we *really* perceive God. This may be a bit difficult because it requires taking off our masks and being completely vulnerable with our most intimate thoughts, feelings and experiences about God, which, by the way, is the completely wrong way to go about developing a true knowledge of God. But we want to look deep into our innermost thoughts, feelings and experiences about God to see how we end up with a false view of God. Have you ever had any thoughts like these?

- *God, I feel like You have forgotten me . . . do You even see me . . . do You care?*
- *God, are You there? You seem so distant.*
- *God, why did You allow him [her] to die?*
- *God, do You not care about my desires? I feel so alone.*
- *God, why did You allow him to rape me? The images will not leave my mind.*
- *God, do You exist? I don't think You do.*
- *God, why did You create me with a disability? This isn't fair. I want to talk and walk and speak like everyone else.*
- *God, I never want to talk to You again because You've really let me down.*
- *God, You could have stopped my parents from getting a divorce . . . why didn't You come through for me?*
- *God, she was too young to die . . . why did You allow that to happen?*
- *God, why don't You care about my desires . . . I wanted him to be my boyfriend forever . . . the man that I was going to marry.*
- *God, why did You cause my father to abandon us?*
- *I am frustrated with You, God.*
- *I am mad at You, God.*
- *I don't like You right now, God.*
- *You've let me down.*
- *This isn't fair, God.*
- *I don't love You anymore.*
- *You have been the one to destroy my life.*

Have you ever had honest thoughts like these about God when something happens that you cannot control? We tend to blame God. The God we may have trusted at one time has become the God who is distant and seems so far away from what is going on now in our broken hearts.

- *Where is God when I need Him?*
- *Where is God in the midst of suffering?*
- *Where is God in the midst of division?*

- *Where is God in the midst of confusion?*
- *Where is God in the midst of crisis?*
- *Where is God in the midst of unfulfilled dreams?*

When I was 18, I traveled with my father to India. This was my first overseas missions trip and I had actually taken an entire semester off from college to make this journey. I was so excited and couldn't wait to land in Mumbai. I had studied the history of India, as well as the culture, and I became extremely fascinated as well as heavily burdened for the people there who had no idea who Jesus Christ, God's Son, really is and the life they could have in Him. I spent a lot of time in prayer before this trip, and I just knew God was going to do great things.

Before the trip, I had read the biography of Amy Carmichael, an 18-year-old missionary to India in the 1800s. I was greatly inspired by her testimony. When we landed, I remember saying to the Lord, "Okay, Jesus, here we are; let's do it! I know You are going to do great things. Use us to evangelize this nation!" I stepped off the plane, went through baggage claim and out of the airport. It was in that moment when all of the excitement I had experienced seconds before drowned in a sea of depression and horrible darkness. I looked into the emptiest, most distant faces I have ever seen in my life. A mother with her infant child began to follow me, pulling on my hair from behind, begging for food. Several orphans began begging for food. People were lying on the ground with no home to go to. There were dead bodies, literally, in my path. It's an understatement to say that I saw extreme poverty.

I wish I could tell you that I just began to rejoice in the Lord; but I did not. I felt so angry with God inside and I began to tell Him about it. He knew anyway, right? *God, why did You do this? This is so cruel, so unfair, so dark. Why did You create India this way? Why are You not providing food and shelter for these people? This is not fair. Are You there, God?* He then began to speak into my honest heart: "Monica, when I created the world, it was perfect; I did not create this."

It is very easy to embrace a false view of who God is when we see things we do not like, or when circumstances cause us to blame the God who loves us in the midst of a fallen world that we, humankind, have created. If I fail to see the reality that exists because of sin (life in a fallen world), I will simply see God as someone who has allowed bad things to happen to me, and not as the God He is—the God who cares about me. I will begin to develop bitterness and hatred toward the One who created me and loves me and has a unique purpose for my life.

If I see God as someone who loves me unconditionally, then I will see myself as someone who is lovable. If I see God as someone who is gracious to cover my sins, then I will see myself as someone who is forgiven. If I see God as someone who made me uniquely, then I will see myself as someone who has purpose. If I see God as someone who has a plan for me, then I will see myself as someone who has hope. As you can tell, the way we perceive our Maker has a direct result on the way we perceive ourselves and the world.

From Head to Heart

If we desire to have an accurate view of God, we must be completely honest with the thoughts we have about Him. He is truth, and He desires that we be truthful. He also desires that we fill in our partial view of who He is.

Because I grew up in a pastor's home, I thought I understood who God was, and I thought I knew where I was going when I died. It was not until I was 13 years old that I realized I had spent my entire life looking at others and hearing about their decisions to follow Jesus Christ without ever examining my own heart. Talk about wearing a mask! I was the queen of masquerades.

When others would make commitments to follow Christ, I would see such drastic changes in their lives, and I thought it was great! However, I didn't realize that I was in need of God and that I had a sin problem like everyone else. My perception of where I thought I would spend eternity was different from the reality, because I truly didn't know where I was going when I died. I had never smoked, drank or been promiscuous, but I was just as much in need of Jesus as anyone could be.

My father was preaching a revival service at a church in North Carolina when I realized for the first time in my life that I had head knowledge about God but no relationship with Jesus Christ. I began to cry in the car on our way home from the revival service, expressing my need of something real and asking my father the question: *Who is Jesus?*

While sitting in the car after we returned home, my father took me through the Scriptures and explained to me who Jesus Christ is and how He could come into my life. He took me through what is called the "Romans Road," an excellent way to walk someone through Scripture to a true and saving knowledge of Jesus Christ, God's Son. He tenderly shared with me the following unchanging truths that helped me understand the reality of who God is, which wasn't what I had perceived Him to be.

1. There is no one who is perfect. We are all in need of God. "For all have sinned and fall short of the glory of God" (Rom. 3:23).

2. If I continue to live a life apart from Jesus Christ, the only thing I have to look forward to is death—a depressing thought, but reality. The good news is that God offers me a free gift of eternal life. There is absolutely nothing I have to do on my own merit to accept His gift of salvation. "For the wages of sin is death, but the free gift of God is eternal life in Christ Jesus our Lord" (Rom. 6:23).

3. In my most sinful state, God died for me. He doesn't wait for me to clean myself up and then accept me;

He accepts me just as I am. He died for me when I was at the lowest and ugliest point in my life. "But God shows his love for us in that while we were still sinners, Christ died for us" (Rom. 5:8, *ESV*).

4. The resurrection of Jesus Christ is what proves He is still alive. He is real! "Because, if you confess with your mouth that Jesus is Lord and believe in your heart that God raised him from the dead, you will be saved" (Rom. 10:9, *ESV*).

5. God offers His gift of salvation to everyone! If you ask Him to come into your life, He will! "For 'everyone who calls on the name of the Lord will be saved'" (Rom. 10:13, *ESV*).

6. Jesus Christ cleanses us from all our sins and gives us peace as we accept Him by faith. "Therefore, since we have been justified by faith, we have peace with God through our Lord Jesus Christ" (Rom. 5:1, *ESV*).

7. After Christ comes into my life, I am free from my past. I am not condemned, but free in Christ. He gives me a new name and a new identity. In essence, my journey of walking in the reality of who He created me to be begins. "There is therefore now no condemnation for those who are in Christ Jesus" (Rom. 8:1, *ESV*).

8. Absolutely nothing can separate me from the love of God. "For I am sure that neither death nor life, nor angels nor rulers, nor things present nor things to come, nor powers, nor height nor depth, nor anything else in all creation, will be able to separate us from the love of god in Christ Jesus our Lord" (Rom. 8:38-39, *ESV*).

After going through these Scriptures, I prayed to ask Jesus Christ to come into my life and forgive me of all my sin. This began my journey of walking in *my identity unmasked*. In 2 Corinthians 5:17, Paul declares, "Therefore, if anyone is in Christ, he is a new creation. The old has passed away; behold, the new has come" (*ESV*). When I placed my trust in Jesus Christ, I became a new creation. Jesus Christ gave me a new name. I discovered my true identity in Him.

Our identity unmasked begins with knowing Jesus—not just knowing Him with head knowledge like I had when I was younger, but also knowing Him in a real, personal way. You begin the journey of knowing God personally by asking Him to come into your life and forgive your sins. He becomes your Savior and makes you into the girl or woman He designed you to be in the very beginning of time. This is the beginning of an adventure of understanding that He is the Creator and Designer of *you*, and He knows what is the very best for you in every way!

Is your identity unmasked and defined by Jesus Christ? Perhaps you have come to a realization that He is not real in your life. Perhaps you have possessed head knowledge of who He is, like I once did, but have never entered into a relationship with Jesus Christ.

Perhaps you haven't had any knowledge at all about Him but have discovered more fully who He is and want to ask Him into your life today. Perhaps you have been filled with an incorrect ideology about God and have realized you haven't ever had a true relationship with Jesus.

I don't know where your heart is today, but God does. The truth is that you may not even know where your heart is today, but God does. If you want to ask Jesus Christ to come into your life and begin the journey of discovering who He has created you to be, then you can pray this prayer out loud or in your heart. You can write out your personal prayer to the Lord in the space on the following page.

Dear Jesus,
I want to know who You are and who You have created me to be.
Please give me a new identity in You. Show me who You are and
who I am. I realize that I have sinned against You and have
walked in my own identity and not Yours. Forgive me for going
my own way. Forgive me from all of my sins. I place my trust
and faith in You and am asking You to come into my life and
give me a new identity. I believe in You and am in need of You.
Thank You for hearing my prayer and coming into my life. Give
me strength to walk with You every day and learn more about
who You are and the purposes You have for me.
In Your name I pray, amen.

YOUR PRAYER

What Do You Think?

What false perceptions has this chapter revealed to you that you have had about God?

_____

_____

_____

_____

_____

Why is it so important to see God for who He is in Scripture, instead of basing your perceptions about God on your experiences?

_____

_____

_____

_____

What is the difference between living by faith in God and relying on your feelings?

_____

_____

_____

_____

_____

Describe a time in your life when you questioned God or wondered if He was really there.

_____

_____

_____

_____

_____

Who is God, based on what His Word says?

_____

_____

_____

_____

What are the eight Unchanging Truths found in the book of Romans that give you a true view of who Jesus is and how you can have a relationship with Him?

_____

_____

_____

_____

_____

_____

_____

Do you have an identity unmasked, defined by a relationship with Jesus Christ? If so, describe what it means to have an identity unmasked. If not, what is keeping you from asking Jesus Christ to forgive you of your sins and come into your life?

_____

_____

_____

_____

_____

Why is discovering who God is so important?

_____

_____

_____

_____

Unchanging Truths to Read and Treasure

PSALM 119:47
ISAIAH 40:25
JOHN 1:1-5
2 CORINTHIANS 6:14
HEBREWS 11:1-3,6
1 JOHN 5:2-3

Note
1. A. W. Tozer, *The Knowledge of the Holy* (New York: Harper Collins, 1961), p. 71.

SECTION TWO

Idolatry
Unveiled

*But I am afraid that as the serpent deceived Eve
by his cunning, your thoughts will be led astray from
a sincere and pure devotion to Christ.*
2 CORINTHIANS 11:3, *ESV*

*The essence of idolatry is the entertainment of thoughts
about God that are unworthy of Him.*
A. W. TOZER

Whatever you love more than God is your idol.
D. L. MOODY

CHAPTER FOUR

Why Can't Life
Be "Utopia"?

*Therefore, just as through one man sin entered the world, and death
through sin, and thus death spread to all men, because all sinned.*
ROMANS 5:12

*This is the message which we have heard from Him and declare to you,
that God is light and in Him is no darkness at all.
If we say that we have fellowship with Him, and walk in darkness,
we lie and do not practice the truth.*
1 JOHN 1:5-6

Sir Thomas More wrote the book *Utopia* in 1516, describing a make-believe island in the Atlantic Ocean that characterized the ideal socio-politico-legal system. Ever since, the word "utopia" has been associated with the most ideal of societies; but in real life it is only a dream for the imagination—a make-believe land somewhere only in the most optimistic of dreams. We could conclude, therefore, that there never has been a true Utopia. Did such a utopian society ever exist in reality?

Imagine the most perfect place possible. What would this place look like? For a woman, this place would represent the deepest form of security and the truest form of love. It would be a world of joy, and free from pain and sickness. This would be a place of acceptance, with no fear of ever being rejected. This would be a world of belonging, exempt from loneliness and insecurities. This perfect place would be the extreme opposite of the world we live in—perhaps a lot like the Barbie doll world I created when I was a little girl, or the world you would escape to while growing up.

This would be a place where our needs would be met and our desires would be granted—a world where contentment, fulfillment, pleasure, harmony, love, happiness, joy, provision, protection, security, belonging, identity, purpose, order, innocence, shamelessness and peace would reign forever in our hearts. What a world that would be!

Within the deepest places of the heart of every woman there is a desperate longing for something more than our world offers. There is an inward compulsion to escape to a place of extreme "utopia." John Lennon wrote about the world he would like to see in his album *Imagine*, released in 1971. You probably know the lyrics: "Imagine there's no heaven, it's easy if you try; no hell below us, above us only sky."

Lennon associated a utopian society as a world without religion and possessions; he saw these things associated with conflict and division. Based on his lyrics, he longed for a better place than the world in which he lived.

Lennon was not the only individual who longed for a different kind of place. Remember the movie *An American Tail*? Released in

1986, it depicts the story of a family of mice who become separated from one another and seek to survive in a new country. The song "Somewhere Out There" in the film was sung between two mice siblings who could not find one another. They were definitely longing for a place where they would be together again and possess a sense of love and security. Take a look at the lyrics: "Somewhere out there beneath the pale moonlight, someone's thinking of me and loving me tonight."

In 1963, an American journalist named Betty Friedan wrote *The Feminine Mystique*. In this book, which helped initiate the first wave of modern feminism, she pointed out women's dissatisfaction in life because they didn't really know who they were. Friedan believed that if women would focus on an education and a career, rather than their role of wife and mother, they would be free from oppression, and experience satisfaction. It is evident that Friedan longed for a better place for herself and for other women, although she believed the answer was found only in becoming better educated and entering the workplace.

Although the world we long to escape to may not seem to exist in the here and now, it did exist in the then and there. The "safe place" that every woman and young girl longs for did indeed exist. In fact, this safe place was woman's first home: *the Garden of Eden*.

When God Gave Mankind Paradise

The Garden of Eden was by far the most utopian (in the sense of ideal) of all societies. We can only imagine what it must have been like to live in a place with no pain, no conflict and no confusion. Yet, we know from the Scriptures that these were, indeed, some of the many wonderful characteristics of this true paradise.

God, the Creator, uniquely designed Adam and Eve's first home to be enjoyed to the fullest. Who else knew better than He in designing this perfect place? The Designer of the world understood more than anyone else the deepest longings and desires of both man and woman, for He created them.

Genesis 1 introduces us to the Creator of the world as He literally creates something out of nothing. Life was nonexistent; there was only darkness and void. "In the beginning, God created the heavens and the earth. The earth was without form and void, and darkness was over the face of the deep. And the Spirit of God was hovering over the face of the waters" (Gen. 1:1-2, *ESV*).

In the midst of absolute nothingness, God pronounced something into nothing. He spoke "Let there be light" into the darkness, and there was light (v. 3). In many respects, "void" is a very difficult word for our finite minds to comprehend, because we cannot imagine what the world was like prior to creation. However, if we relate the word "void" to what it feels like when we are walking through confusing and troubling seasons of life, we can relate without much effort. Who doesn't understand what it means to feel alone sometimes, to feel forgotten, worthless, aimless and lost? In this way, all of our lives can reflect on what existed before God created what we now know as the world and all that is in it and surrounds it.

If you think about it, you will agree that we are all "without form and void" before the God who created something out of nothing transforms us. We are all without an identity unmasked before Jesus Christ gives us a new name. This same Creator-God that we read about in Genesis 1 literally speaks something into your and my nothingness. In other words, He gives meaning to our lives.

God Separated Darkness from Light

Genesis 1:2 tells us that the Spirit of God was also present in the beginning of time: "And the Spirit of God was hovering over the face of the waters" (*ESV*). God's presence was before the beginning of time. His existence has always been. This fact is very difficult to grasp. And we will never understand this truth in its entirety, for we are finite and He is infinite. We are limited in what we can fully comprehend.

When I read Genesis 1:2, it makes me think of the majesty and splendor of the Maker and Designer of everything good. It reminds me of how powerful He is and how aware He is of everything we go through in life. The triune God—Father, Son and Holy Ghost: the Majestic One—has always existed. He has no beginning and no end.

After God created light and called it good, He separated the light from the darkness. It is interesting that even before the first sin took place, God separated light from darkness. These two have always been polar opposites. God created us to be in the light. This is why we face such difficulty if we truly are in the light but we begin flirting with darkness: "This is the message we have heard from him and proclaim to you, that God is light, and in him is no darkness at all. If we say we have fellowship with him while we walk in darkness, we lie and do not practice the truth" (1 John 1:5-6, *ESV*).

Whenever I begin to journey in any direction opposite from God's plan for my life, I become a lie. I don't just start living a lie or embracing a lie, I become someone I was never intended to be. This makes me a lie. A lie is the opposite of the truth. When I lie, I am putting on a mask. I begin living life with an identity that is *masked* rather than an identity *unmasked*. Whenever I seek to be someone I was never meant to be, I begin to practice idolatry. All idolatry begins with becoming something you were never meant to become. Idolatry is when you grow discontent with God, and your affections begin to shift off of your Designer and onto other things (idols).

Solomon said, in Proverbs 23:7, "For as he thinks in his heart, so is he." In other words, what we truly believe can always be seen by how we live; and how we live is always a product of what we believe.

So, dear friend, be honest with yourself; are you living a lie?

God's Timing Is Everything

After we have been given an identity unmasked and we begin to walk in the light, we often come face to face with certain temptations that put our faith to the test. Often, we give up during the test that was intended to make us stronger, and the darkness of our old identity begins to look so appealing. We see something that we think we lack, so we delve into the darkness. Can you relate? It is at this point that we forget who God is and who we are. We make choices that we later regret, and the consequences often stay around for years.

It is easy to lose hope when our focus turns downward instead of upward. All we can see is what we do not have. We forget who we are, and most importantly, we forget who our Creator is—the One who has given us an identity unmasked.

The first solo I ever sang was "In His Time." Are you familiar with this song? "In His time, in His time, He makes all things beautiful in His time." When I sang this song as a five-year-old, I had absolutely no idea the Lord would remind me of this title many times as I grew older, and it would become a principle I would seek to live by. Even later, it would be sung on my wedding day. Often the Lord places in our hearts biblical principles we don't quite understand at a young age, and then they are brought to full bloom as we mature. Or perhaps we really do understand when we are young and accept everything by faith, but as we grow older, we begin to doubt or question.

I have often wanted something in my life that I didn't have yet. I'm sure you have too. So many single girls I speak to today are praying for God's best in their future husband. Here's what one girl said:

> I am 19 years old and waiting on His choice; however, often I grow discontent in my singleness. Frustration really pops out because it hasn't been until recently that I began to desire my future husband like I do now. If all of these emotions would just leave, I would be fine.

Have you ever said or thought something similar to her words, "If all these emotions would just leave, I would be fine"? It's so important to realize that although emotions can complicate things, God gave us our emotions, and they have a good purpose! Keeping our emotions under His control and trusting in Him can be difficult at times. However, waiting on His timing should always be our main focus.

A desire of the heart that hasn't yet come to pass alters our focus. Scripture tells us, "I adjure you, O daughters of Jerusalem, that you not stir up or awaken love until it pleases" (Song of Sol. 8:4, *ESV*). When we seek to awaken emotions or love apart from God's leading, we are missing out on His best during that particular season of our lives. This is just one of the many ways we allow our focus to shift and begin following our own path versus God's plan for our lives.

It's so easy to be distracted at times from the light and turn toward the darkness. The commandments God gives us are never intended to keep us from the best, but to guide us for the best. First John 5:3 reminds us, "For this is the love of God, that we keep his commandments. And His commandments are not burdensome."

We read more about the Creator of light in the book of Genesis. He spoke the entire universe into existence. The same God who spoke something out of nothing has magnificently created you. He has created you to walk in the light, not in the darkness. He has created you to worship Him, and no other.

Man and Woman—the Crown of God's Creation

After God spoke everything else into existence, He created Adam and Eve on the sixth day of creation. We can learn so much about God and our identity by looking at how they were uniquely created.

In Genesis 2, we see the order of creation and the significance of the way God designed both male and female. God is a God of order. He had a purpose in the way He created everything. He had a purpose in the way He created you.

The first people to enjoy God's utopian society were Adam and Eve. God specifically created them on the sixth day, after He had designed the rest of creation. In other words, He built Adam and Eve's home before He created them to live in it. Although Adam and Eve were created in God's image, thus experiencing true equality, God designed them differently from one another for a purpose.

As we probe into the differences between Adam and Eve, recorded in Genesis 2, we will begin to see God's magnificent, intentional design, as well as the utopian society that Adam and Eve experienced as they embraced who they were created to be.

Adam's Identity

In Genesis 2:7-8, we are introduced to the creation of Adam: "Then the LORD God formed the man of dust from the ground and breathed into his nostrils the breath of life, and the man became a living creature. And the LORD God planted a garden in Eden, in the east, and there he put the man whom he had formed" (*ESV*). It is important for us to see both the *order* and the *design* in reference to the creation of Adam. Remember: God intentionally designed the world. He has a reason for everything He does!

There are eight significant factors about Adam (and Eve) concerning Adam's identity unmasked. These factors will aid us to better understand how intentional God was in the way He designed the world:

1. God created Adam *before* Eve (see Gen. 2:7-8,15; 1 Tim. 2:13).
2. God created Adam *equal* to Eve (see Gen. 1:26-27).
3. God created Adam and Eve to have *dominion over creation* (see Gen. 1:26,28).
4. God *blessed* Adam and Eve (see Gen. 1:28).
5. God told Adam and Eve to *procreate* (see Gen. 1:28).
6. God created Adam *differently* from Eve (see Gen. 2:21).
7. God created Adam with a *need* for Eve (see Gen. 2:18, 20,24; 1 Cor. 11:8-9).
8. God created Adam with *dissimilar tasks* from Eve's (see Gen. 2:15-16).

Order: God Created Adam Before Eve

We discover a key characteristic of our Creator God when we read about the way He designed the world. Perhaps the most significant aspect about God in Genesis 1–2 is that He is a God of *order*. He designed the world in six days and created specific things in a distinct order. We know from Genesis 1 that He created humankind on the sixth day. He waited until the last day to create Adam and Eve; and Eve was the last creation to be designed by God.

It is extremely important to see the significance in the order of creation in Genesis 1–2. Genesis 2:7 reveals, "And the LORD God formed man of the dust of the ground, and breathed into his nostrils the breath of life; and man became a living being." Note that Adam was not created in the Garden—he was actually created outside of the Garden, and then placed in the actual Garden by God: "The LORD God planted a garden eastward in Eden, and there He *put* man whom He had formed. . . . Then the LORD God took the man and *put* him in the garden of Eden to tend and keep it" (Gen. 2:8,15, emphasis added). This is completely different from his counterpart, Eve, who was created *in* the Garden of Eden. Only after Adam was placed in the Garden did God cause a great sleep to come upon him, and as he slept, God created Eve.

After Adam was formed, and before the creation of Eve, we understand from Genesis 2:9, "And out of the ground the LORD God made every tree grow that is pleasant to the sight and good for food. The tree of life was also in the midst of the garden, and the tree of the knowledge of good and evil." God made provision for His creation, as well as *choice*. The choice I'm referring to is the choice to obey or disobey God's design . . . His order . . . His paradise.

God never forces anyone to believe that His way is best. He gives us a picture-perfect world in Genesis 1–2 to help us see His design and to understand more fully that His way is best. However, He still leaves the decision up to us to yield to His truth or deny it. The choice is found in Genesis 2:16-17: "And the LORD God commanded *the man*, saying, 'Of every tree of the garden you may freely eat; but of the tree of the knowledge of good and evil you shall not eat, for in the day that you eat of it you shall surely die'" (emphasis added). God specifically gave Adam boundaries for his protection in this perfect world. He also tells Adam the reason why he should stay away from the tree of the knowledge of good and evil: "For in the day that you eat of it you shall surely die." Death would result from any type of alteration or attempt made by man to go against *the order* and design God had created.

The fact that God is a God of order, and He specifically designed Adam before Eve is not only revealed to us in Genesis 1–2, but the apostle Paul also brings up this fact again in the first century. "For Adam was formed first, then Eve" (1 Tim. 2:13).

Equality: God Created Adam Equal to Eve

Adam and Eve were equal to one another. The fact that Adam was created first in no way puts Adam on a more "important" list than Eve. It was simply the order, the design and the manner in which God created the world.

Adam and Eve were created in the very likeness of God. They were uniquely designed to reflect the glory of God in a way the rest of creation could. Adam and Eve were created in God's image to reflect His very personhood. They were created with the ability to magnify God by responding to His holiness and acting according to the order in which He designed the world.

Adam was not given more of the likeness of God than Eve, nor was Eve given more of the likeness of God than Adam. Equality defined is equivalent to essence. Adam and Eve were equal in essence because God designed them in a unique way different from the rest of creation. God designed equality between man and woman. Equality, defined by God, has nothing to do with different roles or tasks, but is defined by the personhood of humankind.

Authority: God Gave Adam and Eve Dominion over Creation

Adam and Eve were created with purpose. Even though they were born into a utopian society, they were given responsibilities in their perfect world. One of their roles was to have dominion over the creation God created for them. In essence, God gave a specific order for the first man and first woman, and that specific order was to keep things in order by exercising authority over creation. This is a very important task, as it reiterates the fact that only Adam and Eve were created to resemble the very likeness and nature of God. They were on a different level and scale to the rest of creation. They were equal to one another as human beings: male and female. They were not equal to the rest of creation, but created in a different sphere altogether.

Blessing: God Blessed Adam and Eve

Can you imagine what it must have been like to have the Creator of the world bless you? God favored them more than the rest of creation. They were His pride and joy. We are told that we will be blessed by God when we follow His precepts: "Blessed is the man who walks not in the counsel of the ungodly, nor stands in the path of sinners, nor sits in the seat of the scornful; but his delight is in the law of the LORD and in His law he meditates day and night. He shall be like a tree planted by the rivers of water; that brings forth its fruit in its season, whose leaf also shall not wither; and whatever he does shall prosper" (Ps. 1:1-3). Being separate from the world is a result of walking in your new identity. As a result of following God's design, we are promised His blessing. I don't know about you, but I want to be blessed by God!

Fruitfulness: God Told Adam and Eve to Procreate

Adam and Eve were not only to enjoy this utopian society on their own, but they were also to be fruitful and multiply. They were the first human beings to be created, but they were the instrument God used to multiply the earth with His image and likeness. "Then God blessed them, and God said to them, 'Be fruitful and multiply; fill the earth and subdue it; have dominion over the fish of the sea, over the birds of the air, and over every living thing that moves on the earth'" (Gen. 1:28).

Differences: God Created Adam to Be Different from Eve

Even in a utopian society there were differences in the way God created Adam and Eve, as well as differences in function. They were created completely equal, yet different. Adam was given specific roles unlike Eve's specific roles, and vice versa. In regard to the creation of Adam, we are told in Genesis 2:7 that God "formed man of the dust of the ground, and breathed into his nostrils the breath of life; and man became a living being." In the formation of Eve, we are told in Genesis 2:21-23:

> And the LORD God caused a deep sleep to fall on Adam, and he slept; and He took one of his ribs, and closed up the flesh in its place. Then the rib which the LORD God had taken from man He made into a woman, and He brought her to the man. And Adam said: "This is now bone of my bones and flesh of my flesh; she shall be called Woman, because she was taken out of Man."

Can you imagine how Adam felt after going into a deep sleep and awakening to the beautiful sight of Eve; someone like him, but noticeably different?

Relationship: God Created Adam with a Need for Eve

God put within Adam's being (heart) the need for Eve. A need goes beyond just a simple desire. Man was created with a real need to be with a woman in the context of God's design and order. Eve was created and designed to be a helper for the man, specifically fulfilling his God-given need. "And the LORD God said, 'It is not good that man should be alone; I will make him a helper comparable to him'" (Gen. 2:18).

Responsibilities: God Created Adam with Dissimilar Tasks from Eve's

God assigned specific roles to Adam before the creation of Eve. These specific roles are found in Genesis 2:15, which reads, "The LORD God took the man and put him in the garden of Eden *to work it* and *keep it*" (*ESV*, emphasis added). At this point, Adam is placed in the garden with these assignments:

- Work the garden
- Keep the garden
- Eat freely from every tree in the garden, but do not partake from the tree of the knowledge of good and evil

First of all, Adam was given the responsibility *to work* the garden. In other words, he was to provide. Whatever the task was, he was to be ready *to give* himself for any reason. Second, he was given the responsibility *to keep* the garden. Adam was to look after and to care for everything in the garden. He was *to guard* and defend everything God had entrusted to him. Finally, Adam was given the command not to eat of the tree of the knowledge of good and evil. Again, Adam was the one that was given this command, before the creation of Eve. He was the individual God put in charge *to guide* his equal partner, Eve, not to eat of the tree that God had forbidden.

You may be saying, "What does any of this have to do with Eve if she had not been created yet?" Due to the fact that *Eve was created in the garden*, Adam would also have the responsibility to *care for her* and to *guard her*, as well as to *guide her*. She had not been given the command not to eat of the tree of the knowledge of good and evil. Most assuredly, this was Adam's responsibility and in keeping with his leadership to convey the importance of obedience.

Although Adam had everything he wanted, he had no counterpart to enjoy life in the Garden of Eden with him. Although created in the image of God, Adam was not God's equal, or even close to it. The Lord created Adam with a need for a counterpart, *someone like him in equality but different in function*:

Then the LORD God said, "It is not good that the man should be alone; I will make him a helper fit for him." Now out of the ground the LORD God formed every beast of the field and every bird of the heavens and brought them to the man to see what he would call them. And whatever the man called every living creature, that was its name. The man gave names to all livestock and to the birds of the heavens and to every beast of the field. But for Adam there was not found a helper fit for him. So the LORD God caused a deep sleep to fall upon the man, and while he slept took one of his ribs and closed up its place with flesh. And the rib that the LORD God had taken from the man he made into a woman and brought her to the man. Then the man said, "This at last is bone of my bones and flesh of my flesh; she shall be called Woman, because she was taken out of Man" (Gen. 2:18-23, *ESV*).

Eve's Identity

After God created Adam's counterpart, he named her "woman." She was part of him and equal to him. She represented something to Adam that he had never seen in any of the rest of creation. Remember, there was no "helper" to be found for Adam. When Eve was created, he recognized her likeness to him, but he also recognized her differences: she shall be called "woman." God created two human beings in His likeness, but He purposefully created them as *different in gender*.

Eve was created to be a subordinate partner to Adam. She was to serve in the role as helper, encourager, confidence builder and promoter. She was created to be a strong support to Adam. She was not created to tear him down or damage his sense of manhood, but to esteem him and believe in him as only a wife could.

At times, women may find it very difficult to understand the specific needs men have, especially in regard to their need for a "helper." It's important to point out that God created Adam with this need. It is also important to point out that just as we may not always understand the needs of man, they also do not understand our needs as women. They may not understand why we feel the need to have their arms wrap around us at times to help us feel secure; they may not understand why we may desire their undivided attention at times, or why we need to be loved unconditionally, or even why it's important to us that they say "I love you" frequently. Whether or not we understand why men function the way they do, it is up to us to be the woman God has created us to be.

Adam and Eve knew they were alike in their equal standing before God, but they also experienced the joys of being different. This is seen even in the name given by Adam to Eve when he first looked at her and said, "Woman." He could have said, "Man." But he didn't. Although completely equal, Adam and Eve were not created to engage in the same tasks. In God's order and design, He specifically gave each of them specific tasks and purposes. The tasks and purposes for each gender are of equal significance. The role of leader is not a higher role to helper; the role of helper is not a higher role to leader.

Uniquely Female

So, what does it mean to be a woman, designed and defined by God, as Eve was? Although this question at first glance may seem trivial and ridiculous, there can be so much confusion in today's culture as to what this really means.

- What does it mean to be a *girl*?
- What does it mean to be *female*?
- What does it mean to be a *she*?
- What does it mean to be a *woman*?
- What does it mean to be a *lady*?
- What does it mean to be *feminine*?

All of these questions have everything to do with our identity unmasked as females. Being a woman is part of the way God designed us; thus, it is part of our uniqueness. Our identity as women is part of how we are defined by God. So who we are is partially linked to our gender identity, in that God specifically created and designed you to be a woman, not a man.

I don't know about you, but I often fall prey to society's view or idea of what a woman is or what a woman should be. It's easy to become mesmerized by the world's view of womanhood through all of the images we see when we flip through a magazine or listen to the voices of the media or popular music. The world's view of what it means to be a woman is the extreme opposite of God's view. Wouldn't you much rather focus on God's design for you and allow His truth to permeate your mind and heart?

Let's look at two biblical principles that can change the way you think about yourself as you walk through this world.

Principle 1

Being a woman isn't defined by what you do or like, but by the fact that God created you specifically to be a woman.

I was recently teaching a class of all-female college students. At the beginning of the course, I asked them to share their names as well as hobbies or activities they enjoyed. I wanted to get to know them a bit more personally in class. One young woman, after stating her name said, "Well, I am no 'girlie' girl. I like to play sports and do guy stuff." This class was a women's survey course to discover what God's Word declares about biblical masculinity and femininity. So I pointed out the obvious that was overlooked in this student's description of herself.

"Good," I responded. "Nothing wrong with playing sports. But you are a woman."

The student looked back at me and said in a reluctant yet hesitant manner, "Yes." I was once more reminded of the stereotypes our culture places on masculinity and femininity. Although both men and women play sports and are good at sports, for some reason we link sports to men more than women. Because of this, many girls who excel at sports see themselves as unfeminine. We have a tendency to define femininity in reference to what we do and what we like mixed in with stereotypical views instead of defining it as the essence of our being, which God intentionally created.

The essence of who we are and were created to be as women is our femininity. This should be something we treasure, not something we reject. Many women reject their femininity due to a lack of understanding of what it really means to be a woman, whether it is by embracing more masculine activities and proclaiming we are not "girlie" girls, or embracing the latest trends through plastic surgeries and cosmetics to enhance our appearance of what a beautiful, sexy, girlie woman "should" look like.

We live in a society of extreme confusion on the essence of femininity. If you have a desire never to wear makeup, or you wouldn't dare leave your house without your lipstick or other cosmetics, the fact that you are a woman can never be denied, even though most of the time our culture defines it inaccurately. Who am I to be as a woman?

PRINCIPLE 2

Being a woman isn't defined by feeling accepted by men but by the fact that my Creator God accepts me and has created me to be a woman, different from man.

Again, being female doesn't mean that you like or dislike things that are viewed as being "girlie." The meaning of being female goes much deeper than the stereotypical analysis pronounced on gender.

Many women today often go against their gender identity because they want to be accepted by guys. To gain their attention, they begin liking the things guys like, regardless of whether or not they enjoy it. Men can often unconsciously dishonor women in regard to their gender identity. And women can do the same to men. For example, have you ever watched a movie and burst into tears because something moved you emotionally? A gripping scene touches your heart and you begin to literally sob your eyes out? At that moment, you find yourself connected to a story other than your own; it becomes personal to you because you connect to your circumstances and experiences.

All of a sudden, you hear a whisper in your ear from the guy next to you: "Are you seriously crying?"

You feel like saying, "Um, no, Mr. Wise Guy, I just put fake tears in my eyes. What does it look like?"

He then says, "You are being such a girl!"

Has that ever happened to you? Perhaps you have heard a "cousin" remark while playing a game of basketball or softball. You happen to be the pitcher on the softball field, and a guy screams out, "Don't throw it like a girl!" Comments like that are not only stereotypical but can be degrading and damaging to self-worth and gender identity as a female.

Women long for acceptance and, at times, can even deny their natural design, to be accepted by men. I played softball when I was in the fifth grade, and I was absolutely awful at it; but I do have female friends who are incredibly great softball players. Although they are great at the sport, they are still girls. Girls can be good at sports just like guys. We should not necessarily categorize our femininity apart from athletics; however, we should also never deny the natural design given to us by our Creator.

I challenge you: Instead of allowing comments such as these to steer you away from anything feminine, next time, stand up and remind others that you are a girl. You are a woman, and that is how your Designer created you! Women need to embrace their uniqueness rather than fall into the temptation to be who they are not. Again, femininity should not be defined by embracing what we name stereotypical "girlie" activities versus "guy" activities. (For an example—Girlie Activities: shopping, facials, manicures, pedicures, or the color "pink". Guy Activities: sports, hunting, fishing, anything but the color "pink.")

Regardless of your likes and dislikes, never define the essence of who you are (your gender) based on your interests. Your true femininity can be seen in the difference in the creation of Adam versus Eve, as well as specific role assignments designed by God for women to primarily fulfill. You were created equally to a man, differently than a man and with the primary task of being a helper and support.

A biblical definition of womanhood is clearly portrayed in Genesis 1–2, as we observe Eve's identity unmasked: designed by God; made in the image of God to resemble her Maker; equal to her male counterpart but different in the essence of her feminine design and function. These unchanging truths characterize what it means to be a woman defined by God:

1. I am created by God = God is my Creator.

2. I am created in the image of God = God created me in His image.

3. I am created to have dominion over the rest of creation = God created me to have dominion over the rest of creation.

4. I am created both similarly and dissimilarly to a man. I am similar in reference to being created *equal* to a man, in God's image = I am dissimilar in reference to my gender and function (purpose) than a man. I am different biologically and in regard to my specific purpose.

The Creator and Designer of you is God. As you embrace Him as your Designer, you are acknowledging and accepting His plan for you as a woman and can begin walking out your identity unmasked, just as Eve was created to do!

A True Love Story

The relationship Adam and Eve experienced was greater than any you could ever hope for in a romance novel. Think about it: Eve was created in a resort of resorts, and there Adam was, waking up from a long nap. Adam looked up, oblivious to the fact that he had a need for a helper (in Genesis 2:18, the text reveals that God said it was not good for a man to be alone; this conveys that God knows our needs before we know our needs).

Upon waking, he saw the most beautiful creature he had ever laid eyes on. She was the only woman in Adam's life, for she was the only woman created at this point. God didn't give Adam several women to choose from; He brought Eve specifically to Adam (see Gen. 2:22). This was Adam's counterpart, his helper. He was a one-woman man in every way. Their bodies were perfect and they had complete innocence, absolute peace with God, and His blessing and provision. The union they experienced was one of absolute love and respect.

Can you imagine how good Eve had it? No other woman to be jealous of or to compete with. She had Adam's pure and complete devotion. Genesis 2:24-25 records, "Therefore a man shall leave his father and his mother and hold fast to his wife, and they shall become one flesh. And the man and his wife were both naked and were not ashamed." Although Genesis 2:24 mentions father and mother, it tells us what we experience as sons and daughters of Adam and Eve. They had no earthly father and mother. This Scripture also conveys the act that was experienced by Adam and Eve, and what is to take place between a man and woman in marriage.

What is the point here? What's the big deal about Adam and Eve in this passage that makes this a "utopian" place? Think about it . . . *Adam knew who He was as a man. Eve knew who she was as a woman. They both knew their identity unmasked and therefore were able to function in a complete and healthy relationship.* Eve was not seeking to find out who she was or gain her worth in Adam; nor was Adam seeking to gain who He was in Eve, as we so often do today. They both knew who they were. They were *equal* but *different.*

Both Adam and Eve knew who they were and had access to the very best in the Garden. Adam knew what it meant to be a man, and Eve knew what it meant to be a woman. They were not ashamed in their relationship, and they experienced wholeness, pleasure and complete harmony. Can you imagine?

Adam   Eve

God specifically created Adam to be male, and He specifically created Eve to be female. God's design for marriage has always been between a man and a woman. If it were to be any other way, He would have designed human relationships differently. Adam and Eve not only had a perfect relationship with one another, but they also had a whole relationship with their Creator. Can you imagine the closeness of their relationship with God? They had nothing hindering the way they related to one another and to God, and they lacked nothing. Talk about a true utopian society—this was it!

Let's look at the description below of the utopian society Adam and Eve enjoyed in the Garden of Eden:

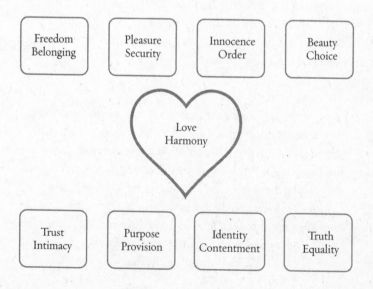

Although Genesis 1–2 describes a utopian society that was real, it is quite obvious that we no longer live there. The key principle for us to understand in this chapter is that when God created the world, it was perfect, and He created both Adam and Eve with a choice to obey or to disobey His design and order.

In the next chapter we will see more clearly how Adam and Eve abandoned their identity and began to wear masks. Although created to live in a utopian society with God, Adam and Eve made the choice to disobey God, and now you and I live in a fallen world. We experience the opposite from life in a utopian society, due to sin. The apostle Paul declares, "Therefore, just as through one man sin entered the world, and death through sin, and thus death spread to all men, because all sinned" (Rom. 5:12). We suffer the consequences of sin each and every day of our lives; but that doesn't mean there's no hope! Jesus said, in John 6:35, "I am the bread of life. He who comes to Me shall never hunger, and he who believes in Me shall never thirst." He is still a God of order even if we choose to live in the chaos and darkness of sin.

Have you ever blamed God for pain you have experienced? Have you ever accused Him for all the wrongs people do? Have you grown discontented with who God is because you have started to flirt with the darkness again? Remember: God created the world perfectly. It is because of sin that we live in a fallen world, not because God doesn't care.

Dear Lord,
Forgive me for losing sight of the truth that when You created the world it was perfect. Forgive me for blaming You for the sinful world I live in. I need Your help to live out my identity unmasked as a woman You formed. Thank You for creating and designing me as a woman for a reason and a purpose. Forgive me for pretending to be someone I was never created to be. Strengthen me to see You for who You really are. May I take joy in how You designed me as a woman.
In Your name I pray, amen.

YOUR PRAYER

_____
_____
_____
_____
_____
_____
_____
_____
_____
_____
_____
_____
_____

WHAT DO YOU THINK?

Describe what a perfect place would look like to you.

_____
_____
_____
_____
_____

What kind of place did God create in the very beginning of time?

_____
_____
_____
_____
_____

Why do you think God created such a perfect paradise?

_____

_____

_____

_____

Why do you think the world is no longer "utopia"?

_____

_____

_____

_____

What was Adam and Eve's "identity unmasked"?

_____

_____

_____

_____

What does it mean to be a woman by God's definition?

_____

_____

_____

_____

Have you ever been confused at the meaning of "femininity"? If so, describe.

_____

_____

_____

_____

What are two principles that help define what femininity is not?

_____

_____

_____

_____

_____

Unchanging Truths to Read and Treasure

GENESIS 1:1
PROVERBS 23:7
SONG OF SOLOMON 8:4
ROMANS 5:12
2 CORINTHIANS 11:3
1 JOHN 1:5-6; 5:3

CHAPTER FIVE

Once Upon a Time:
Masquerade Revealed

*For since by man came death, by Man also came the resurrection of the
dead. For as in Adam all die, even so in Christ all shall be made alive.*
1 CORINTHIANS 15:21-22

*Do not be deceived, God is not mocked; for whatever a man sows, that he
will also reap. For he who sows to his flesh will of the flesh reap corruption,
but he who sows to the Spirit will of the Spirit reap everlasting life. And let
us not grow weary while doing good, for in due season we shall reap if we
do not lose heart. Therefore, as we have opportunity, let us do good to all,
especially to those who are of the household of faith.*
GALATIANS 6:7-10

I was a freshman in college and thought for sure that I had met the man of my dreams. He was tall and handsome and had dark hair. Just the package I had been waiting for! He also happened to be both an athlete and a Christian. Well, I thought he was a Christian. After leaving a public school, he was the first guy of such caliber that I had encountered, or so I thought. In my mind, it couldn't get much better. I was hopelessly head over heels!

During the first week of classes, the "guy of my dreams" asked me for my phone number. I was unaware that he had also asked about five other girls. We ended up going out a few times, but never alone. We would hang out with other friends and acquaintances. The more I got to know him, the more red flags shot up. But instead of admitting to his many character and integrity flaws, I began to overlook them. Why? Because I had chosen not to guard my heart, and I slowly began to take my focus off of Christ and put it onto this possible relationship. I was gradually becoming deceived by not submitting my desires to my Designer and Maker. Have you ever been deceived? Have you ever forgotten your Creator God and placed your affections in a different direction?

When I saw so many red flags, I should have run in the opposite direction. The Bible is so clear on the unchanging principle that believers are not to have romantic relationships with unbelievers. Paul tells us, "Do not be unequally yoked together with unbelievers" (2 Cor. 6:14). But what did I do? I continued to get more and more attracted to him.

As my interest in him increased, I became even more emotionally attached. In spiritual terms, I had become extremely rebellious, because I was very aware of his character issues, yet I decided to overlook everything that bothered me. I was full of desires and thoughts for and about him that would not leave. Although we had never held hands, kissed or anything else, my heart was entangled with someone I should not have been hanging out with—not even for a moment.

Monica Rose Brennan · www.regalbooks.com

Ignoring the Voice of the Holy Spirit

During these days of deceiving myself, I continued to faithfully have my devotional times. I read God's Word, wrote in my prayer journal, prayed, attended church and participated in outreach events. However, these spiritual disciplines seemed to become more and more difficult to do. Others perceived me as a strong Christian, but on the inside, I was in great distress. I definitely was wearing a mask. There was no true joy in my life. As I read God's Word, the Holy Spirit would speak to my heart, convicting me that I didn't need to spend time with this guy. The Holy Spirit began revealing to me that I was deceived.

At this point, I entered the most dangerous stage of deception. I began to literally ignore the conviction of the Holy Spirit, which had become so strong when I had my devotions that one day I realized I could no longer read the Bible. I was walking in disobedience. My desires and affections were shifting from Christ to another direction. God became so distant, and my good days were solely dependent on whether or not I had had a conversation with "Man of my Dreams."

It was during this time that I was asked to travel with the president of the college I was attending, to sing before he would speak. I also was asked to be a part of a traveling team that went into different churches and held ministry rallies and events. We would sing and do drama as a ministry and outreach to the church and community. I knew my "spiritual state" was not that of an influential Christian, so I stepped down from being a part of this ministry traveling team. Shortly before I stepped down, I was asked to hold the position of prayer coordinator for all the ministry teams on campus. What a privilege to even be considered for such a role! However, because of the difficulty I was having spiritually, I said no to this ministry opportunity.

I became extremely discouraged in my spiritual walk. I could no longer hear God's voice. He seemed so far away, and I didn't feel like He really cared anymore. As I focused more and more on the affections of my flesh instead of Christ and the needs of others, I remember getting to the point of desperation and literally crying out to God to speak to my heart.

One day, I decided that I couldn't take being in such misery anymore. Enough was enough! I wanted so desperately to have my joy back. I took an old blanket and went outside behind my dorm room where no one could see me. I spread out the blanket and sat down with my Bible and my prayer journal. I was determined not to leave until God helped me. Three hours later, I didn't feel a thing. Why was God so distant? Why didn't He care?

Over time, I realized that God had been there the entire time, but I had willfully allowed sin to come into my life. I chose to listen to the Deceiver. I could not hear the wisdom from God through His Word because I was walking in deception, and sin was present in my life. I had forgotten who I was. I had forgotten my true identity and had begun to live in idolatry. I had allowed this guy to shape my identity. My beliefs and convictions about Jesus Christ became secondary.

You could say that I was the unhappiest Christian girl you would ever meet. I still belonged to God; I was still His daughter, and He still loved and cared for me; but I had chosen to go a different way than the one God had created me to walk on. I had begun to live a life of idolatry.

Living a Lie

Idolatry is simply forgetting who God is and who you are. Idolatry is placing your focus, affections and priorities on someone or something in place of God. Idolatry is when God is no longer first in your life. I chose to shift my focus from God and His precepts to something else that I thought I needed. *I forgot who I was and who my Creator is.* I began living a lie and putting on an act.

Many of us have been living a lie for so long that we are completely unaware that we are putting on an act. While we may know our personality well, we are clueless about our personhood. When we no longer walk in truth, we walk in falsehood.

We read in Galatians 5:16, "I say then: Walk in the Spirit, and you shall not fulfill the lust of the flesh." The apostle Paul exhorts us in this verse to walk in our newfound identity. When we begin living life in the flesh (our old identity apart from Christ), our focus turns to self, and we no longer have the one who is truth leading us; rather, we lead ourselves. We follow the path that seems right in our own eyes. In Galatians 5:17, Paul tells us, "For the flesh lusts against the Spirit, and the Spirit against the flesh; and these are contrary to one another, so that you do not do the things that you wish."

When I began to embrace a lifestyle of idolatry as a freshman in college, I began to wear a mask and slowly become someone I was never intended or created to be. My actions were completely contrary to the lifestyle God created me to live.

As I continued to forget my Maker and my God, I experienced extremely low times. My entire life evolved around obtaining attention from "Man of my Dreams." My belief system shifted. I overlooked the red flags. I justified his behavior and my behavior. I had become what I once hated: a pretender. I told everyone I was fine, but on the inside, I was miserable. I needed help. I needed truth. I needed to be reminded of who I was and to whom I belonged.

Although I felt lonely, rejected and forgotten, it was the result of my own choices. I was simply reaping the consequences of idolatry. In Galatians 6:7-10, Paul says, "Do not be deceived, God is not mocked; for whatever a man sows, that he will also reap. For he who sows to his flesh will of the flesh reap corruption, but he who sows to the Spirit will of the Spirit reap everlasting life. And let us not grow weary while doing good, for in due season we shall reap if we do not lose heart. Therefore, as we have opportunity, let us do good to all, especially to those who are of the household of faith."

As the Lord began to show me how deceived I was, I chose once more to obey Him. I didn't "feel" the idolatrous desires or emotions leave all at once, but I knew I was pleasing God. The decision to turn away from this possible relationship was not easy, but God gave me strength to walk in His ways again as I confessed my sin of idolatry.

Can you relate to this story? Perhaps you are going through something similar right now.

A Utopia of the Heart

In Genesis 3, we read about the first woman, Eve, who also experienced deception. She lived in utopia, but something happened to this perfect society God had uniquely created for intimacy with Him and one another. Something had changed.

What changed can be described in a word: "idolatry." You become an idolator when you forget who God is and who you are—when you place your focus, affections and priorities on someone or something other than God.

Adam and Eve, who experienced true utopia, received the consequences of their sin. And as a direct result, we experience the same. We are now fallen creatures born into a world that is the opposite of utopia.

I have good news for you: Although we cannot go back to the Garden of Eden, the Creator and Designer of that world desires to make our hearts a place where He can dwell. You can experience utopia in your heart here on earth by walking in your true identity. You can be filled with absolute peace by experiencing your identity in Christ. We read in Galatians 5:24-25, "And those who are Christ's have crucified the flesh with its passions and desires. If we live in the Spirit, let us also walk in the Spirit."

So what happened to turn this place of utter delight into a place of absolute disappointment? Let's be reminded once again.

Assuming a False Identity

What keeps us from living out our identity in Christ? What keeps us entangled and mesmerized with the world's idea of us more than God's view of us? What do we allow to creep into our lives in subtle ways that keep us living life in a masquerade? Again, in one word, the answer is idolatry. Walking in the flesh (our old identity) versus walking in the Spirit (our new identity in Christ). We see this contrasted in Galatians 5:19-23:

> Now the works of the flesh are evident, which are: adultery, fornication, uncleanness, lewdness, idolatry, sorcery, hatred, contentions, jealousies, outbursts of wrath, selfish ambitions, dissensions, heresies, envy, murders, drunkenness, revelries, and the like; of which I tell you beforehand, just as I also told you in time past, that those who practice such things will not inherit the kingdom of God. But the fruit of the Spirit is love, joy, peace, longsuffering, kindness, goodness, faithfulness, gentleness, self-control. Against such there is no law.

We first read about idolatry in Genesis 3. Adam and Eve took their thoughts and affections away from being enthralled with their Father and put them onto their fleshly desires that were aroused through an openness to sin. We are introduced to what sin looks like and the progression of temptation in Genesis 3:1-6:

> Now the serpent was more crafty than any other beast of the field that the LORD God had made. He said to the woman, "Did God actually say, 'You shall not eat of any tree in the garden'?" And the woman said to the serpent, "We may eat of the fruit of the trees in the garden, but God said, 'You shall not eat of the fruit of the tree that is in the midst of the garden, neither shall you touch it, lest you die.'" But the serpent said to the woman, "You will not surely die. For God knows that when you eat of it your eyes will be opened, and you will be like God, knowing good and evil." So when the woman saw that the tree was good for food, and that it was a delight to the eyes, and that the

tree was to be desired to make one wise, she took of its fruit and ate, and she also gave some to her husband who was with her, and he ate (*ESV*).

We can clearly see the progression of sin in the first 6 verses of Genesis 3. As Eve forgets her true identity, she begins to gradually put on layers of masquerade (masks) that hide who God created her to be. Four masks are evident in the life of Eve and portray how subtly sin occurs in the life of any believer when she takes her focus off of Christ and walks in her old identity.

Adam and	Masquerade 1: DECEPTION
Eve's	Masquerade 2: DOCTRINE SHIFT
Disobed-ience	Masquerade 3: DESIRE
SIN	Masquerade 4: DECISION

Deception: The First Layer of Eve's Mask

We have a tendency to read over Genesis 3 in such a flippant manner that we come away from the text thinking, *Eve, how could you have been so foolish to eat from a tree?* It is so much easier to point a finger at others and their faults. However, when we are faced with a certain temptation, our feelings may be quite different.

I don't believe Eve's choice to disobey God took place in a matter of seconds. It's not like she woke up beside Adam and thought to herself, *I think I will just blow it today and destroy the amazing relationship we have with each other.* Sin takes on the form of something so subtle that we can easily be deceived. That is why it is so important to take guard against Satan and be aware of his devices (see 2 Cor. 2:11).

We read in 1 Peter 5:8-9, "Be sober, be vigilant; because your adversary the devil walks about like a roaring lion, seeking whom he may devour. Resist him, steadfast in the faith, knowing that the same sufferings are experienced by your brotherhood in the world." Just as your Designer passionately desires you to walk in truth, so too the father of lies, the devil, desires you to walk with a mask on— your entire life, not knowing who you are or who your Maker is.

Jesus was having a conversation with a group of people who were basically saying that God was their Father, but they were not walking in God's truth. Here's what He told them:

> If God were your Father, you would love me, for I came from God and I am here. I came not of my own accord, but he sent me. Why do you not understand what I say? It is because you cannot bear to hear my word. You are of your father the devil, and your will is to do your father's desires. He was a murderer from the beginning, and has nothing to do with the truth, because there is no truth in him. When he lies, he speaks out of his own character, for he is a liar and the father of lies. But because I tell the truth, you do not believe me. Which one of you convicts me of sin? If I tell the truth, why do you not believe me? Whoever is of God, hears the words of God. The reason why you do not hear them is that you are not of God (John 8:42-47, *ESV*).

Satan will say anything to make us go against our Maker and forget who we are in Christ. It is the father of lies who deceptively made his way to Eve. This was the first war in human history between darkness and light. Interestingly, the attack was not on Eve but was a direct assault on the Father of light, the Creator of the world, the Designer and Maker of all the earth and humanity.

The fact that the serpent attacked Eve before going to Adam is very significant. Many would suggest that the serpent attacked Eve because she was weaker; such a statement could not be further from the truth. She was a complete equal to Adam and an educated woman as far as life in the Garden was concerned. Eve's education on sin is evident in her response to the serpent. She knew she was not to eat of the fruit of the tree of the knowledge of good and evil. The serpent attacked Eve instead of Adam to assault the *order* God had specifically placed in creation. Remember, God created Adam first. Satan was at war, and is still at war, with the Author of Order: "For God is not a God of confusion but of peace" (1 Cor. 14:33, *ESV*). By approaching Eve first, Satan was assaulting God's design and order for the entire world.

As the father of lies entered into a conversation with her, Eve became confused in her thinking and her emotions. Our actions are always influenced by what we believe. Obviously, Eve was allowing her emotions and desires to dictate her reaction to the serpent. Instead of looking to her Father God, from whom she had unconditional love and security, her attention drifted to the lowest of all creatures. We read in Genesis 3:1 that the serpent was craftier than any of the other animals. The enemy approached Eve in great deceit, yet disguised himself as an extremely intelligent creature—so intelligent that he basically told Eve that God didn't know what He was talking about.

Satan's deceit in the *form of a serpent* was the first mask ever worn by anyone. Satan disguised himself as an intelligent, persuasive creature, representing ultimate desire. His Mask of Deception spoke so subtly but directly to Eve that he influenced her to wear a mask as well. The mask of deception Eve put on covered up who her Designer created her to be and the purpose He had for her life.

When the Master of Deception (Satan) literally began to speak to her, Eve had not yet completely entered into deception. However, when she began to respond to the serpent instead of walking away, she became radically engaged in his illusion. What appeared to be something harmless was actually something that would lead to her death. Instead of living out the truths given to her by her Maker, she began living out a lie. She literally forgot God's purpose for her life. She forgot that God was present with her. She forgot that God was her Designer, and He had uniquely and purposefully created her. She forgot that God loved her and cared for her like no other. Eve forgot her true identity and the fact that she was marvelously made!

She began to forget all of these truths as she entered into Satan's deception. Remember Genesis 1:28, where God commands both Adam and Eve to have dominion over the rest of creation? Eve had dominion over the serpent. Yes, he may have been the craftiest of the beasts of the field, but she had control and mastery over him. The moment she began her conversation with the serpent was the moment she began to forget who she was.

We read in James 4:7-10, "Therefore submit to God. Resist the devil and he will flee from you. Draw near to God and He will draw near to you. Cleanse your hands, you sinners; and purify your hearts, you double-minded. Lament and mourn and weep! Let your laughter be turned to mourning and your joy to gloom. Humble yourselves in the sight of the Lord, and He will lift you up." Talk about equality! Woman was the first creature to lower herself—to lower her standing. Her discussion was with a creature not her equal. She gave in to something she was created to have mastery over.

When we look around us through the eyes of deception, what we once would have resisted becomes appealing and desirous—just as I was deceived when a freshman in college with "Man of my Dreams." Lust begins to form in the once-captured soul and passions rise so rapidly that you can hardly stop them. You seem to be led in a different direction than your passions have ever taken you before. You see something you don't think you can live without, and it engrosses your attention, crying out, "This can give you pleasure!" The key for the Christian woman to remain steadfast is to pray for discernment in every matter of life. We fail as Christian women if we do not act on our discernment. "Therefore, to him who knows to do good and does not do it, to him it is sin" (Jas. 4:17).

The first step of walking in deception for a Christian woman is when she begins to question her Maker's design of her, just as

Eve began to listen to the lies of the serpent. Eve was at the wrong place at the wrong time and began flirting with darkness. She made the choice to give in to deception, just as we do at times when we begin to question the identity of God Himself.

We take our focus off of God—the one who cares for us the most—and get mesmerized with an idol that appears to fulfill our desires more than Christ. Deception says, "This person, place or thing can bring me more pleasure than Christ." God's Word says, "Grace and peace be multiplied to you in the knowledge of God and of Jesus our Lord, as His divine power has given to us all things that pertain to life and godliness, through the knowledge of Him who called us by glory and virtue, by which have been given to us exceedingly great and precious promises, that through these you may be partakers of the divine nature, having escaped the corruption that is in the world through lust" (2 Pet. 1:2-4).

Let us take heed to the passage in 2 Corinthians 11:3, which reads, "But I am afraid that as the serpent deceived Eve by his cunning, your thoughts will be led astray from a sincere and pure devotion to Christ" (*ESV*). We have all we need in Christ!

Doctrine Shift: The Second Layer of Eve's Mask

The second action Satan took with Eve was to question her entire belief system. He accomplished this by creating doubt in her mind regarding her Maker. "Did God actually say, 'You shall not eat of any tree in the garden'?" (Gen. 3:1, *ESV*). In this question alone we discover how very deceptive Satan was toward Eve. He approached her with a question he knew was not true, to create a discussion. She didn't have to respond, and she had no business speaking to a creature over which God had given her dominion. However, she made the choice to enter into a conversation with the Great Deceiver. Eve's response was, "We may eat of the fruit of the trees in the garden, but God said, 'You shall not eat of the fruit of the tree that is in the midst of the garden, neither shall you touch it, lest you die'" (vv. 2-3, *ESV*).

Satan attacked God's provision in his first question. Of course, they could eat from the fruit of the trees. God had created the trees for food to eat. The one thing God said to stay away from, Satan zeroed in on and made a huge deal of it. To use a modern example, this would be like Satan saying to you, "You mean God never wants you to have sex?" or, "God wants your life to be miserable as a Christian; there is no fun when you follow Christ."

In Genesis 3, Satan was basically making God look like an absolute miserable Father, ruling with strict orders to make life in the Garden unbearable. Through his question, he was subtly making this paradise and utopian society look as if it was not beautiful. Satan created discontentment in Eve's heart, just as he creates discontentment in our hearts. It is our choice to take our focus off of our Creator and begin worshiping a creature that was never intended to have our attention or conversation.

Has your belief system in God ever shifted? Have you ever believed that God's character was something it is not? Have you ever been tempted to go your own way, take your own path? Have you ever compromised the truth of God's Word with an erroneous set of beliefs so that you could do your own thing?

Satan targets our mind and thoughts to get us to believe things that are not true about God:

- *God doesn't care about me.*
- *God doesn't really hear my prayers.*
- *I am not special to anyone.*
- *There is no hope for me in God.*

All lies! We must recognize the lies as they enter our mind and dismiss them immediately. Eve should have done this, but she did not. Why would she not immediately recognize that these were lies about God's identity? To put it simply, her desires were aroused by what the serpent was promising her. Have your desires ever been aroused to the point of not being able to think clearly?

Desire: The Third Layer of Eve's Mask

For a woman, deception can grow at a rapid pace whenever her emotions are involved. Although God created us with emotions and desires, we are to keep our hearts guarded and wait on God for each and every decision we make. For example, when we open up our heart and mind to a person we know isn't God's best for us, we begin to practice idolatry once again. We are placing our affections above God's plan.

After the serpent told Eve that she would not die if she took of the fruit, he appealed to her emotions and desires. We read in Genesis 3:4-6, "Then the serpent said to the woman, 'You will not surely die. For God knows that in the day you eat of it your eyes will be opened, and you will be like God, knowing good and evil.' So when the woman saw that the tree was good for food, that it was pleasant to the eyes, and a tree desirable to make one wise, she took of its fruit and ate." Before Satan offered Eve a plateful of "desires" to appeal to her open and gullible heart, he literally called God a liar: "You will not surely die."

God had promised Adam and Eve that if they partook of the fruit of the tree of the knowledge of good and evil, they would die (see Gen. 2:17). Satan attacked the very personhood and nature of God, and Eve began to listen and eventually believe the lie as truth.

Eve's belief system was altered due to the desires Satan offered her. What did he offer Eve? He used four desires, and choosing them ultimately resulted in the death of mankind: Satan offered the lure of (1) *equality*: to be like God; (2) *security*: to be taken care of; (3) *beauty*: to be beautiful; and (4) *wisdom*: to be wise (see Gen. 3:5-6).

Idol #1 = *Equality*: to Be Like God

Satan appealed to Eve's contentment in being who she was created to be. Eve was created in the likeness of God, different from the rest of creation. Satan appealed to her desire for more power and dominion than God had given her. As she gave into this desire, she began to worship *the idol of power*. Satan had promised Eve something he could not give her, thus fulfilling his role as a liar.

Idol #2 = *Security*: to Be Secure, Taken Care of

The greatest need a women has is not only to know who she is (identity) but also to know she belongs to someone (security). Eve's need for security was evident when Satan lured her to believe that the tree represented something that was "good for food." Eve began to worship *the idol of security*. But wait! Didn't Eve already have security in Christ? All of her needs were met in this utopian society. Satan offered Eve something she already had; but due to her deception, she could no longer see clearly.

Idol #3 = *Beauty*: to Be Beautiful

Men are not the only ones who struggle with things that appeal to the sight. The tree "was pleasant to the eyes" (Gen. 3:6). Satan deceived Eve with the desire for something that symbolized beauty. This isn't surprising to me, because so many of us strive to be beautiful and will do whatever it takes, at times, to feel like we are appealing in the eyes of others. Eve was already a beautiful creation of God and lived in the most beautiful of homes. Again, Satan was offering Eve something she already had. But due to her deception, she could no longer see clearly. Eve began to worship *the idol of perfection*, although she already lived in a perfect place.

Idol #4 = *Wisdom*: to Be Wise

When Satan offered Eve wisdom, her desires for more had already been aroused, although she had it all! In accepting Satan's logic, Eve literally became the most foolish woman. We read in Proverbs 14:1, "The wise woman builds her house, but the foolish pulls it down with her hands." Due to Eve's idolatrous desires, she ruined the perfect home God had made for her and for her husband. Eve began to worship *the idol of wisdom*.

Decision: The Fourth Layer of Eve's Mask

Eve's identity became masked to the extreme as she made the ultimate decision to give in to the lies of the deceiver. As Satan offered Eve the four deadly desires, Genesis 3:6 says, "She took of its fruit and ate. She also gave to her husband with her, and he ate." This is a very revealing verse of Scripture, because it indicates Eve's forgetfulness of her identity, her change in what she believed (doctrine), her desires apart from Christ, and now her decision to go against God's plan and order. Although this may have been a spontaneous decision for Eve, it wouldn't surprise me if it were something she had contemplated before giving in to the many lies of the Deceiver. Perhaps Eve experienced thoughts such as these as she was debating what to do:

"No one will ever find out."

"This really isn't a big deal."

"Why would God give me these feelings if He didn't want me to enjoy life in the Garden?"

"I have so much love and desire in my heart for these things. This must be from God."

"I just can't say no, so I might as well enjoy it."

"I am way too serious about God's instruction."

"God is not real."

"This experience will actually make me smarter."

"I really need this in my life."

Eve most likely had a lot of different thoughts as she was conversing with the serpent. After she took of the forbidden fruit, she gave some to her husband, Adam, and he ate of the fruit as well. The serpent influenced Eve, and then she influenced her husband who was standing beside her during her decision. Talk about a world of order turned into a world of disorder, this was it!

If we have sin in our lives, we cannot make decisions clearly because we lack discernment, just like Eve. Paul wrote in 2 Timothy 3:6 how false teachers have a form of godliness and lead women "loaded down with sins" in the wrong direction. It's important for us to see in this passage that it is easy for Satan to lure us deeper into his trap when we have sin in our lives. Here's the rest of this passage:

But know this, that in the last days perilous times will come: for men will be lovers of themselves, lovers of money, boasters, proud, blasphemers, disobedient to parents, unthankful, unholy, unforgiving, slanderers, without self-control, brutal, despisers of good, traitors, headstrong, haughty, lovers of pleasure rather than lovers of God, having a form of godliness but denying its power. And from such people turn away! For of this sort are those who creep into households and make captives of gullible women loaded down with sins, led away by various lusts, always learning and never able to come to a knowledge of the truth (2 Tim. 3:1-7).

Adam's False Step

When Eve decided to take of the fruit, Adam's decision was to be silent and fail to fulfill his leadership role given to him by God. Instead of being a giver to Eve, Adam became a withholder. He was with her but did not step in to help guide her in the right direction or help her make the right decision. Instead of influencing Eve, he allowed her to influence him. Instead of being a guard for Eve, offering protection, he attacked her. He literally blames the sin on Eve and, ultimately, on God Himself.

Once upon a time, Adam walked in his true identity. He knew truth and walked in the truth. Once upon a time, Adam lived in the image of his Father. Once upon a time, Adam knew who he was as a man. When he forgot his Maker's instructions and who he was created to be, he began to experience an identity crisis. Instead of fulfilling one of the primary purposes God had given him in leading his wife, he began to follow his deceived and disillusioned "helper."

Eve did not listen to her husband. She did not stay away from the tree of the knowledge of good and evil. Instead of walking in her true identity, she believed the lies of Satan. Instead of being the helper she was created to be for her husband, she became the greatest hindrance to Adam. Instead of helping Adam be the man of God He was created to be, she literally handed him poison. Our sin always influences others.

Once a
Giver, Guard and *Guide,*
now a
Withholder, Attacker
and *Follower*

Once a
Helper,
now a
Hindrance

Adam   *Eve*

Once Upon a Time . . .

After Adam and Eve sinned against God, Scripture reveals six results of their disobedience:

- **Result #1: *Devastation*** —Any time we make a decision to go against God's plan for our lives, the result will be devastation. Adam and Eve were devastated by the loss of their perfect relationship with one another and also with God.

- **Result #2: *Desperation*** —A once authentic relationship turned into one characterized by shame. Adam and Eve hid themselves from one another and from God.

- **Result #3: *Death*** —Death resulted from Adam and Eve's sin against God (see Gen. 3:21; Rom. 6:23).

- **Result #4: *Departure*** —Adam and Eve had to leave the utopia of the Garden. And we now live in a fallen world.

- **Result #5:** *Depravity*—Adam and Eve were left with an ultimate need for God. Now all of humanity is in need of a Savior, who has promised to give us hope in this fallen world. His grace is available to all who place their trust in Him.

- **Result #6:** *Destruction*—Adam and Eve's relationship was destroyed due to sin, and God punished both of them.

The moment they tasted the poison, Adam and Eve become *devastated*: "Then the eyes of both were opened, and they knew that they were naked; and they sewed fig leaves together and made themselves coverings" (Gen. 3:7). Adam and Eve were ashamed. After they "gave in" to what they thought was going to bring them greater fulfillment, they realized how horrible the poison really tasted. Their devastation led to *desperation* as they tried to cover themselves by sewing fig leaves together to make clothes for their bodies.

Immediately after Adam and Eve sinned against God, they were aware of their idolatry. In an attempt to cover up their shame, they began to hide. Once upon a time they enjoyed the freedom of innocence, but now they found themselves in bondage to their own shame.

At this point, the masks Adam and Eve were wearing became more and more heavy. They knew they were going to have to experience *death,* and they were trying their best to hide from God: "And they heard the sound of the LORD God walking in the garden in the cool of the day, and the man and his wife hid themselves from the presence of the LORD God among the trees of the garden" (Gen. 3:8). Once upon a time, God's presence was Adam and Eve's delight; now, in their desperation to hide their sin, they ran from their Father.

The layers of their masks became even thicker as they literally blamed God for their sin. In the midst of Adam and Eve's false identity, which led to completely irrational behavior and utter confusion, we see their Maker as the one who is still in control over all of His creation. In spite of the direct assault on the utopian society He had created, God is still a God of *order*. Even sin could not strip God from His glory or the way He designed the world. This is first seen as God calls for Adam: "Then the LORD God called to Adam and said to him, 'Where are you?'" (Gen. 3:9).

You may be saying, "Well, what's the big deal about that?" Well, Eve was the one who gave Adam the poison, right? You would think God would have asked for Eve first, but He did not. He approached Adam first, because he was the first human to be created, and he was the one responsible for guiding Eve. Although Satan sought to destroy the divine order, God held everything together in spite of the sin of Adam and Eve. God was ultimately conveying that there had been an assault on His creation, but He was still the Author and Finisher of His world, and it would still bring Him glory.

God's calling after Adam has much significance to apply to our own lives: God was still a God of order as He called for Adam, not Eve; God held Adam responsible because He created Adam with the purpose to guide and lead Eve; and God was indicating that He still wanted a *relationship* with Adam. He chose to communicate and seek out Adam, although Adam sinned against Him (see Gen. 3:9).

Where Is Your Heart?

Has anyone—perhaps your closest friend or a family member—seen right through your disguise? Sometimes a best friend or a parent can see directly through what we are hiding, because they know us and love us the most. When God asked Adam, "Where are you?" He was not referring to a location, but to Adam's heart. He was basically asking, "Where is the Adam I created?" "Where is your true identity?" Perhaps you have had someone say to you, "Where are you?" We know they are not referring to where we are standing, but rather to where we are in our heart. They see a change in us that is not normal, and they are deeply concerned.

Have you ever had a conversation with someone when you knew his or her thoughts were somewhere else? In order to get this person's attention, you probably said, "Where are you?" God knew exactly where Adam was hiding and where his heart was. God simply wanted Adam to see his desperate state of need and realize what he had done and what he was responsible for. God was calling out to Adam to remind him of the relationship He still desired to have with Adam. However, before the relationship could be healed, God pointed out Adam's sin.

The Blame Game

Adam realized that God was not referring to a specific location in the Garden. We see this in Adam's response in Genesis 3:10: "And he said, 'I heard the sound of you in the garden, and I was afraid, because I was naked, and I hid myself' " (*ESV*). After Adam responded to God's question, God asked two other questions: "Who told you that you were naked?" and "Have you eaten of the tree of which I commanded you not to eat?" (v. 11, *ESV*). God held Adam responsible and specifically confronted Adam with his sin.

All the while, Adam continued to put on layers of masks. Instead of confessing his sin, he blamed God for his sin. Here's what he said to God: "The man said, 'The woman whom you gave to be with me, she gave me fruit of the tree, and I ate' " (v. 12, *ESV*). Although the woman gave him the poison, Adam was conveying that it was God who created the woman, so it was God's fault. Adam was totally forgetting his ability to make the right choice.

God formed both Adam and Eve with a heart, a mind, a soul and a will. Instead of creating Adam and Eve as robots, He created them with the ability to choose. They had the choice to obey or to disobey. He has created you and me the same way. He has created us with the choice to follow His design or go against His order.

So often when we choose to go our own way instead of God's, we blame our sin on someone else in order to hide our shame. This is not only being untruthful, but it also creates another great hindrance to our discovery of our true identity. Basically, we are creating a deeper and deeper layer of masks on our false identity. Adam's identity was covered up by falsehood. He shifted the blame to someone else. Although Adam was responsible for Eve's behavior, as he was created to be her "guide," he blamed his sin on his Father.

Adam is not the only one who shifted the blame onto someone else; Eve also covered up her true identity with falsehood. After God addressed Eve for offering poison to Adam, she blamed the serpent: "Then the LORD God said to the woman, 'What is this that you have done?' The woman said, 'The serpent deceived me, and I ate'" (v. 13, ESV). It's almost as though Eve is justifying her sin due to being deceived.

Have you ever blamed your sin on someone else?

"I didn't realize he didn't really love me, or I wouldn't have had sex with him."

"He deceived me into thinking he was someone he was not."

"It really wasn't my choice at all; he practically forced me to take the pills."

"I couldn't help it. If they hadn't pressured me to do it, I wouldn't have gotten drunk."

"They said they would never be my friend if I didn't go . . . so, I had to go."

"My mom was the one to drop me off, so really it is her fault this happened."

"But he told me I was beautiful. If he hadn't been so persuasive, I wouldn't have given in."

"Well, if God had not given me this desire, it wouldn't have happened . . . He created me this way, so really it is His fault."

Although someone may deceive us at times, deception is not anyone's fault but our own. Scripture has a revealing passage about who is responsible for giving into deception:

Blessed is the man [or woman] who remains steadfast under trial, for when he [or she] has stood the test he [or she] will receive the crown of life, which God has promised to those who love him. Let no one say when he [or she] is tempted, "I am being tempted by God," for God cannot be tempted with evil, and he himself tempts no one. But each person is tempted when he [or she] is lured and enticed by his [or her] own desire. Then desire when it has conceived gives birth to sin, and sin when it is fully grown brings forth death. Be not deceived, my beloved brothers [or sisters] (Jas. 1:12-16, *ESV*).

Remember the progression of sin outlined in Genesis 3? It all begins with *deception.* Whenever we take our focus off of who God is, we experience great discontentment. Instead of seeing how good we have it in Christ, we see our lack. There will be testing in life. Most assuredly, *our true identity will be tested.* However, tests were not meant to hurt us, but to sharpen us—to help us realize even more who our God is and who we are.

We read in James 1:2-4, "Count it all joy, my brothers [or sisters], when you meet trials of various kinds, for you know that the testing of your faith produces steadfastness. And let steadfastness have its full effect, that you may be perfect and complete, lacking in nothing" (*ESV*). As we learn how to live out our true identity, we will realize that we have everything in Christ. But if we fail to realize our true identity in Christ and take our focus off of Him (idolatry), we will give in to the *desires* that give birth to sin.

Due to God's love for Adam and Eve, even in their sin, He provided a remedy for the destruction that occurred due to their idolatry. He provided a remedy and solution for us as well, if we come back to our Father and begin to believe the truth and live in it.

After Adam and Eve hid from God by wearing fig leaves in an attempt to cover their shame (see Gen. 3:7), God clothed them with tunics of skin as a symbol of the shedding of blood and His *righteousness* as the only way for mankind to come back to Him: "Also for Adam and his wife the LORD God made tunics of skin, and clothed them" (Gen. 3:21). Although we can try to cover up our sin, it is only God's righteousness that can take away our sin and give us forgiveness.

Although this situation looked absolutely hopeless after sin took place, God exhibited a great love for all of humanity in offering His only Son as a sacrifice for our sin to provide *redemption from sin* (see Gen. 3:15). Still, God made sure that the serpent and Adam and Eve understood the consequences of their behavior.

A Curse Upon the Serpent

After Adam and Eve tried to hide from God by shifting the blame for their wrong choices, God confronted falsehood. It's as if God allowed both Adam and Eve to justify their behavior and then He declared both the curse and the punishment. Although God's order and design were directly assaulted, and war transpired, the Creator God still brings forth truth in the midst of falsehood. He continues to bring order out of chaos by addressing the direct attack that occurred in this most perfect utopian society.

God addresses everyone involved in disobedience against His design and He does so in the order in which the sin took place. The first one He addresses is the Mask Maker, the author of falsehood, confusion and deception: Satan. It was Satan who directly attacked the order God created. Satan directly assaulted God and did so by convincing Eve that he was smarter than God and convincing Adam that Eve was smarter than God. Eve listened to the serpent and Adam listened to his wife, though both were clearly going against God's design.

God addressed the assault in Genesis 3:14-15. We see in these verses that God placed a curse on the serpent: "The LORD God said to the serpent, 'Because you have done this, cursed are you above all livestock and above all beasts of the field; on your belly you shall go, and dust you shall eat all the days of your life. I will put enmity between you and the woman, and between your offspring and her offspring; he shall bruise your head, and you shall bruise his heel'" (*ESV*). When God placed a curse on the serpent, he put him in physical discomfort and humility, and He also placed him in a position of absolute and utter downfall. In other words, God put the serpent (Satan) back on his rightful throne, which is on the lowest level imaginable.

Although the Messiah would not come to earth until God's perfect timing had arrived, we are actually introduced to the Savior, God's Son, in Genesis 3:15. The Messiah's mission is foretold in this verse. He would die for humanity and ultimately defeat the Great Deceiver!

God is the Restorer. He established a covenant with his people even though they sinned against Him. He gave them a second chance because of His love for the world! In the midst of Adam and Eve's disobedience, God presented His Son, the Savior. He gave grace in the midst of Adam and Eve's punishment, but proclaimed that Satan would be destroyed.

Let's look at this verse again in Genesis 3:15. It says, "He shall bruise your head, and you shall bruise his heel" (*ESV*). He is talking to the serpent when he is saying that "He" (Jesus Christ) will bruise his head. A bruise to the head is always a mortal wound. Then God says to the serpent that the serpent would bruise His (Jesus Christ's) heel. The heel is foretelling the time when Jesus' heels would be bruised on the cross. Bruises to the heel do not dictate a mortal wound (see Isa. 53).

Consequences for Eve and for All Women

After God curses the serpent, He punishes Eve. Adam and Eve were not cursed; only the serpent and the ground were cursed. Here is Eve's punishment: "To the woman he said, 'I will surely multiply your pain in childbearing; in pain you shall bring forth children. Your desire shall be for your husband, and he shall rule over you' " (Gen. 3:16, *ESV*). There would be severe pain in childbirth, and she would struggle with her role of being a helper to Adam. In her flesh, she would often run away from her God-given role and not appreciate her husband's leadership. She would struggle with her purpose and the role given to her by God.

Consequences for Adam and All Men

After God punished Eve, He spoke to Adam and said, "Because you have listened to the voice of your wife and have eaten of the tree of which I commanded you, 'You shall not eat of it,' cursed is the ground because of you; in pain you shall eat of it all the days of your life; thorns and thistles it shall bring forth for you; and you shall eat the plants of the field. By the sweat of your face you shall eat bread, till you return to the ground, for out of it you were taken; for you are dust, and to dust you shall return" (Gen. 3:17-19, *ESV*).

Adam's sin was that he listened to his wife (who was going against God's design) instead of listening to God. We must remember the order and design in which God created the world. Adam was created first, then Eve. Adam was given the command not to eat from the fruit of the tree of the knowledge of good and evil. Adam was responsible to guide Eve, to lead her. Instead of leading Eve against deception, Adam was silent and literally watched her ingest poison when she ate the fruit. Adam then took the poison from Eve. Because of Adam's sin, not only was he given punishment, but God also cursed the ground.

Men and labor are affected by Adam's sin. Throughout history, men would now have a difficult time with their roles, just as women would have a difficult time with theirs. Men would struggle to provide. What once was given freely to Adam in this utopian society would now cost him greatly. He would have to labor hard to provide for himself and his family.

God Still Has a True Identity for Humanity

God so graciously loved Adam and Eve that He gave them an opportunity to take off their masks. Often we try to hide from God when we sin. However, God is the only one who can cover up our shame and make us into a new creation and give us a true identity. Although once upon a time there was a utopian society, God sent His only Son to give a facelift to the world. His Son would be the restorer of what was broken, and he would bring meaning out of nothingness, and order out of chaos.

Although we do not live in a utopian society now because of sin, we can experience grace and restoration in a relationship with the Savior of the world, Jesus Christ. Although we still live in a fallen world, He enables us to experience true utopia in our hearts. As we experience our true identity in Him, He gives our lives purpose and meaning.

Adam and Eve's relationship is a prime example of what happens when we go against God's order. At the same time, we see God give them so much grace. We also see the restoration of their relationship and bond to one another after sin is confronted. Genesis 4:1 reads, "Now Adam knew Eve his wife, and she conceived and bore Cain, saying, 'I have acquired a man from the LORD.'" Adam knew Eve, his wife, in the most intimate sense. Although they were not back in the Garden of Eden, they were able to taste utopia in their hearts due to the Great Restorer.

We can apply the principles found in Genesis 1–3 to our lives today. Although we are fallen people, God has a plan for our restoration. His order was not destroyed, although a spiritual war did take place, and it continues today. God is still in control in the midst of this world of chaos. And one day, all will come into His perfect order. Until that culmination, God has a plan and an order for all humanity to embrace.

Dear God,
Please forgive me for giving in to any type of deception.
Help me to embrace who You are and
not forget who You have created me to be. Thank You
for the grace You give when I sin against You.
May I follow Your design and order.
Thank You that You are in control in the midst of
the chaos that sin brings into the world.
May I trust in Your plan.
In Your name I pray, amen.

YOUR PRAYER

_____

_____

_____

_____

_____

_____

_____

_____

_____

_____

_____

_____

_____

WHAT DO YOU THINK?

Describe a time when you were deceived and walked apart from God's truth.

_____

_____

_____

_____

What is an idol? Why is idolatry so dangerous?

_____

_____

_____

_____

What happened to the perfect society God created in Genesis 1–2?

_____

_____

_____

_____

_____

What was the tragic result of Adam and Eve's idolatry?

_____

_____

_____

_____

_____

Describe the four masks that were evident in the life of Eve as she forgot her true identity.

_____

_____

_____

_____

_____

How does Jesus describe Satan in John 8:42-47?

_____

_____

_____

_____

_____

Have you ever been at the wrong place at the wrong time, as Eve was? Describe this time in your life and what choice you made.

_____

_____

_____

_____

In what way(s) did God demonstrate His desire to have a restored relationship with humanity after sin entered the world?

_____
_____
_____
_____
_____

Unchanging Truths to Read and Treasure

1 CORINTHIANS 15:21-22
GALATIANS 6:6-10
2 TIMOTHY 3:1-7

CHAPTER SIX

Taking Off the Mask: Unveiling My Idols

Do not turn to idols, nor make for yourselves molded gods:
I am the LORD your God.
LEVITICUS 19:4

And we know that the Son of God has come and has given us an
understanding, that we may know Him who is true; and we are in Him
who is true, in His Son Jesus Christ. This is the true God and eternal life.
Little children, keep yourselves from idols. Amen.
1 JOHN 5:20-21

I will never forget a young teenage girl who attended a camp I was working at one summer. She was sitting on the pulled-out bleachers with her hands covering her face, tears rolling down her cheeks. Her shoulders were shaking. My heart immediately went out to her and I went over to where she was sitting and wrapped my arm around her shoulders and asked her if I could help her in any way. She looked up at me with mascara streaked in rivulets down her cheeks and brokenly murmured, "Yes."

As we walked away from the large crowd, she began to share with me how she had been so excited to attend the youth camp, because she hadn't thought she would be able to come. I asked her why. Her eyes began to fill up with tears again and she said, "Before I left to come here, I found out I was pregnant. I just told my boyfriend the news, and he has been ignoring me all day—he doesn't want to be around me . . . he's not paying any attention to me." She went on to say her friends were encouraging her not to tell her parents that she was pregnant, and they were pressuring her to have an abortion.

This young girl was going through so much emotional turmoil. She had given her body to someone she wanted the attention from, and now he had completely rejected her. She had placed her self-worth in being accepted by her boyfriend. Now, she didn't have his focus and was left in a hopeless situation. She didn't know what to do.

We continued to talk for a long while, and she admitted she had sinned against God and had put her boyfriend ahead of God's plan for her life. She had made him an idol. She wept and wept, and then she repented of her sins.

We kept in touch for a long time after camp. She sent me pictures of her newborn baby that she decided to keep. What was the root issue? My friend had failed to find her complete identity in Christ alone, her Maker. Instead she looked to other people, other places and things, to fill the void in her life.

If you're saying, "Well, I've completely blown it! I've done exactly what that girl did." Perhaps you decided to have an abortion and now you really struggle with that decision. The truth is, we all have blown it! There is nothing in and of ourselves that makes us righteous apart from Christ. But God's forgiveness, mercy and sovereignty are there for the person who seeks it. He longs for His creation to see their worth and realize that all of the attention and acceptance they need is found in Him alone. We must identify the idols in our lives and submit ourselves to God and His plan, which is always the best.

A Divided Heart Is an Idolatrous Heart

There are many passages of Scripture that discuss idolatry, but let's look at Psalm 135:15-18, which says:

> The idols of the nations are silver and gold,
>   the work of men's hands.
> They have mouths, but they do not speak;
>   eyes they have, but they do not see;
> They have ears, but they do not hear;
>   nor is there any breath in their mouths.
> Those who make them are like them;
>   so is everyone who trusts in them.

This passage gives a description of how meaningless idols are and explains that when we worship them, we literally become like them. In other words, as we turn our devotion from Christ and place our number-one affection on something or someone other than Christ alone, we are literally stripping away our true identity, which has been given to us by our Maker.

Idols can appear to be appealing and promising on the outside, but when we trust and worship them instead of our Maker, at some point we realize how meaningless and self-made they really are.

Have you ever felt divided in your heart regarding your relationship with Christ and a path that looks so appealing? Have you ever forgotten your God and turned toward the affections of your flesh?

The moment we take our focus off of Christ as the number-one recipient of our affections, we take our first step toward idolatry.

We are reminded in 1 John 5:20-21 of the importance of understanding who is the true God and our need to keep our lives pure from any other devotion placed ahead of Christ: "And we know that the Son of God has come and has given us an understanding, that we may know Him who is true; and we are in Him who is true, in His Son Jesus Christ. This is the true God and eternal life. Little children, keep yourselves from idols." It is possible to take your eyes off of Christ and become mesmerized with the desires of the world. It's not that other "desires" are necessarily wrong, but they become sin (idolatry) when we place them ahead of Christ, our marvelous Maker, who designed us for a unique purpose.

Let me tell you about a friend of mine who requested to meet with me to discuss an issue that was consuming her thoughts. She was on a women's ministry team that I was leading at the time, but I could tell she had a heavy heart. We met that week at a local coffee shop, and she began to open her heart to me. The conversation went something like this: "Monica, I know how important it is to be real. I don't want to pretend. I just want to be completely up front with you. I can no longer be on this ministry team. I don't want to be a hypocrite. I want you to know that I have made the decision to completely abandon God. I have decided to choose my own way, apart from Christ."

As I sat there listening to her, I felt a lot of mixed emotions. First of all, I felt admiration for her honesty with me. I appreciated the fact that she was not trying to hide her feelings. At the same time, I knew she was being deeply deceived by Satan. I'm reminded of the verse in Revelation 12:10, which states that Satan is "the accuser of our brethren." He wants us to believe his lies, and my dear friend was giving in to the accusation that God's plan for her life was no longer best. As she continued to talk, I began to pray that the Lord would help me show her truth and give me discernment as I shared with her.

After she finished talking, I thanked her for her authenticity and then asked a question that had come to my mind throughout our conversation. "Does this have to do with a guy?"

In a shocked and surprised voice, she shared with me, somewhat sheepishly, that she was in a relationship with a guy who was not a Christian. She knew it was wrong, but she wanted to stay in this relationship more than she wanted to follow Christ. There was no mistaking the idol she allowed to creep into her life. She reiterated the fact that she didn't want to be a hypocrite, and she was making her choice to "abandon God." She shared how, at first, she had tried to be an example to her boyfriend; but then he ended up influencing her more than she was influencing him. He became more important to her than God.

I felt alarm in my heart at the seriousness of what she was saying and the deception the enemy had achieved over her mind. I again thanked her for her honesty and began to remind her of God's unchanging truth. I remember sharing that although she was saying she was going to abandon Christ, He would never abandon her. Once she came into a relationship with Christ, she was God's daughter, and there was no getting rid of Him as her Father. Regardless of the sin she may commit or the deception she accepted, God would never leave her. She may choose to go her own way, but He was still pursuing her to come back to the truth.

Although my sister in the Lord had given in to idolatry (placing other affections and desires above Christ), God's truth for her was so much bigger than her desires. God's truth is that way for all of us, because He *is* truth! What did my friend need? She simply needed to be reminded of who God is and who she is called to be as His daughter. She had forgotten her Maker and began to embrace a life of idolatry by placing her affections for a guy above her affections for Christ. At the same time, she was going against God's Word by developing a romantic relationship with a non-Christian.

I opened my Bible to Psalm 139 and asked my friend to read verses 7 to 12 out loud:

Where can I go from your Spirit?
　　Or where can I flee from Your presence?
If I ascend into heaven, You are there.
　　If I make my bed in hell, behold, You are there.
If I take the wings of the morning,
　　and dwell in the uttermost parts of the sea,
Even there Your hand shall lead me,
　　and Your right hand shall hold me.
If I say, "Surely the darkness shall fall on me,"
　　even the night shall be light about me;
Indeed, the darkness shall not hide from You,
　　but the night shines as the day;
　　the darkness and the light are both alike to You.

She literally began to weep as she clearly saw the magnificence of God up against the miserable "Christian" life she was attempting to live. When you begin to live a lifestyle of idolatry, the end result will always be discontentment. My friend realized how much God loved her, even if she chose to go a different direction. God would never forsake her, because she belonged to Him.

When we allow idols into our life, we miss out on God's best. We can make the choice to go after other gods and idols; but in forsaking our Maker, we leave behind the reality of the person He created and destined each of us to be. Yet, He will never forsake us or give up on us.

When we make wrong choices, God still loves us. One day, in God's timing, He will bring the culmination of all things, and that includes judging all things by the standard of His holiness. For now, He is long-suffering toward us, waiting for us to put our idols aside and live the life He has designed for us. Why would we want to defy His will and go our own way? His way is always best, regardless of how appealing Satan can make other things look.

My friend had simply forgotten who she was in Christ. She had lost her first love and placed her attention on something else ahead of Christ. You may be saying, "Well, what's the big deal about that? What's the big deal about putting something ahead of Christ?" Matthew 6:24 declares, "No one can serve two masters; for either he will hate the one and love the other, or else he will be loyal to the one and despise the other. You cannot serve God and mammon." You and I were created to worship one God. The Great Deceiver wants us to take our attention off of Christ so we will not fulfill God's purpose, plan and dream for our lives.

Even in our weakest times and greatest temptations, Christ gives us strength to overcome any battle. Paul wrote, "And He said to me, 'My grace is sufficient for you, for My strength is made perfect in weakness.' Therefore most gladly I will rather boast in my infirmities, that the power of Christ may rest upon me" (2 Cor. 12:9).

Don't Forget Your First Love

Have you ever taken your focus off of your Marvelous Maker and placed it on something or someone else? Have you ever struggled with temptation? Do you feel like you are being misled at this moment and are turning toward a lifestyle of idolatry? Have you become mesmerized with an affection or desire other than Christ?

It is so important to recognize the idols we allow in our life and repent so that we can fully discover God's plan and purpose for our lives, and glorify Him in how we live. I don't know about you, but I don't want anything to interfere with God's best for my life! Jeremiah 29:11 records God's thoughts about us: "For I know the thoughts that I think toward you, says the LORD, thoughts of peace and not of evil, to give you a future and a hope."

In Revelation 2:1-5, we read about a church that was doing all the right things on the outside but was failing horribly on the inside. What was this church doing that so displeased God? Scripture teaches that they had lost their first love:

To the angel of the church of Ephesus write, "These things says He who holds the seven stars in His right hand, who walks in the midst of the seven golden lampstands: 'I know your works, your labor, your patience, and that you cannot bear those who are evil. And you have tested those who say they are apostles and are not, and have found them liars; and you have persevered and have patience, and have labored for My name's sake and have not become weary. Nevertheless I have this against you, that you have left your first love. Remember therefore from where you have fallen; repent and do the first works, or else I will come to you quickly and remove your lampstand from its place—unless you repent.' "

The church we read about in this passage was doing so many things the right way. They were patient, didn't tolerate evil, labored in the gospel and did not grow weary of doing good. On the outside, you would think this body of believers had it all together. But they were losing sight of the most important thing: loving God. We love God by placing Him first in our lives, with no compromising devotion toward anything or anyone else.

Have you ever been in love? Have you ever thought you were in love? All the feelings, emotions and excitement can make you feel like you are on top of the world! For true love to grow, however, it must be cultivated. When you begin a romantic relationship with someone, you don't just tell him you love him and never spend time with him. In order for that relationship to develop on any level, it takes time, energy and absolute devotion and priority.

I'm reminded of the story of Mary and Martha in Luke 10:38-42:

Now it happened as they went that He [Jesus] entered a certain village; and a certain woman named Martha welcomed Him into her house. And she had a sister called Mary, who also sat at Jesus' feet and heard His word. But Martha was distracted with much serving, and she approached Him and said, "Lord, do You not care that my sister has left me to serve alone? Therefore tell her to help me." And Jesus answered and said to her, "Martha, Martha, you are worried and troubled about many things. But one thing is needed, and Mary has chosen that good part, which will not be taken away from her."

There is so much drama going on in this passage. Martha has lost her focus (her first love) and become distracted. She has become more concerned with serving than being at Jesus' feet. It's important to remember that Martha was a woman of God and had sat at Jesus' feet; however, she left that position as her top priority. Her focus shifted. Jesus reminded her of the one thing—not two things, but one thing—that was necessary: worshiping Him as supreme in her life and loving Him above all else.

When we have Christ as our first love, we will be free from idolatrous living. Just as Martha was distracted and had left her first love, I often get distracted and leave my first love as well. Have you ever done that? Are you there right now?

Safe in Your Father's Arms

One morning, when I entered the kitchen to make some coffee, my father was sitting at the kitchen table and looked very serious, as if he had something important on his mind. He asked me if he could talk to me about something on his heart. When I sat down, he began to share with me a dream he'd had the night before. He believed he was to share it with me as a warning. I have written the dream as he shared it, but in the form of a story.

I felt snugly wrapped in the warmth and protection of my father's strong grip around my tiny hand as we entered the busy airport. "Stay close to Daddy," my father said. In the midst of such a crowd it would be easy for a four-year-old girl to wander off and never be seen again.

As we made our way to the airport terminal, my adventuresome spirit began to awaken. My entire being felt full of desire and energy to run and jump! When my father's eyes looked up for a moment to see the flight destinations on the airport screen, I slipped my hand from his grip and I was gone. I went off to play!

Immediately, my father realized I had left his side. "Monica," he yelled, "come back to Daddy, sweetie."

Was that Daddy's voice I heard? I thought to myself. I turned around and grinned from ear to ear, signaling to Daddy that it was playtime!

She doesn't realize the danger in this. Oh, God, help me not to lose her, my father thought.

I ran around the tall people that seemed like giants to me, having so much fun by myself.

But my father didn't take his eyes off of me as he ran speedily in order to rescue me from the dangers I didn't know existed. "Monica, sweetie, come back to Daddy," he continued to yell.

I would not listen, this was too much fun. I then made a sharp turn and the crowd immediately hid me from my father.

"I have lost her," my father cried. He continued to run on his mission to save me.

His eyes never lost hope to find his wandering, naïve daughter. He made the same sharp turn I had, and there he saw me, but the sight horrified him. I had crawled into a large silver tube. The sand in the tube was beginning to engulf me. My father could only see my head, which was beginning to get buried in the light brown sand. His hands reached for me and pulled my head up out of the sand until my entire being was pulled from the tube. He dusted me off.

My long blonde hair had sand in each bouncy curl, and my large blue hair bow had been removed. My dress, with all its ruffles, was no longer pressed and bright but was wrinkled and dirty.

My father began to wipe away the dirt from my torn dress and the tears of bewilderment from my eyes. He embraced me in his strong, protective arms. "Never run from Daddy again, sweetheart. Daddy can see things you cannot," my father said.

"Okay, Daddy, I'm sorry," I replied. "Never again."

Although this was a dream my father dreamed about me, it serves as an excellent illustration concerning the importance of being identified by the Father, following Him daily and not getting distracted by things that divert our focus from Christ.

I admit that at times I want to go my own way. I want to leave my heavenly Father and do things according to my fleshly desires. I forget who my Father is and what I believe about who He is. I so often forget that He can be fully trusted, because He is who He says He is.

The moment I begin to believe something different about who God is and begin listening to the lies of the Deceiver, I have trusted in a false reality rather than the truth. The falsehood that calls out to me arouses the desires of my heart but is always lacking in lasting satisfaction. The deception that looks so real and fun leads to only more disaster. It is in this moment that I am embracing the world's view of me, instead of God's. It is in this moment that my desires are not one with my Maker's. We no longer have harmony in our fellowship because I am out of tune with the blessings of His will.

When I yield to His way, things seem effortless and He gives me His peace. When I go my own way, there is always defeat, misery and pain. It is crucial to remember that there is safety and security when we follow Christ and do not put other things ahead of Him.

Idols are deceptive in many ways. They can appear to be so appealing. They offer pleasure, but never lasting pleasure. We must choose to walk in our true identity and not give in to the idols of this world.

Moses was reminded of his true identity when he refused to be called the son of Pharaoh's daughter. We read in Hebrews 11:24-26, "By faith, Moses, when he became of age, refused to be called

the son of Pharaoh's daughter, choosing rather to suffer affliction with the people of God than to enjoy the passing pleasures
of sin, esteeming the reproach of Christ greater riches than the
treasures in Egypt; for he looked to the reward."

Have you ever placed something in front of Christ and prac-
ticed idolatry? Hebrews 12:1-2 talks about getting rid of all the
weights, or idols, in our life by setting our focus on what is true:
Jesus Christ: "Therefore, since we are surrounded by so great a
cloud of witnesses, let us also lay aside every weight, and sin
which clings so closely, and let us run with endurance the race
that is set before us, looking to Jesus, the founder and perfecter
of our faith, who for the joy that was set before him endured the
cross, despising the shame, and is seated at the right hand of the
throne of God" (*ESV*).

What Are Your Idols?

What weights, or sins, are holding you back from living the life
your Maker has called you to live? Perhaps several things come to
mind. In the Old Testament, we discover that God had to remind
His people on many occasions not to look to idols, but to the
Lord: "Do not turn to idols, nor make for yourselves molded
gods: I *am* the LORD your God" (Lev. 19:4).

Have you forgotten your identity in Christ? Have you turned
to the idols of this world and forgotten your God? We see in the
Old Testament book of Jonah that idols are worthless. They may
look appealing on the outside, but they never offer lasting satisfaction or security: "Those who regard worthless idols forsake
their own Mercy. But I sacrifice to you with the voice of thanks-
giving; I will pay what I have vowed. Salvation is of the LORD"
(Jon. 2:8-9).

Anything you place before God will negate the purpose for
which He created you, because you were created to worship your
Maker above all else: "Inasmuch as there is none like You, O LORD
(You are great, and Your name *is* great in might), who would not

fear You, O King of the nations? For this is Your rightful due. For among all the wise men of the nations, and in all their kingdoms, there is none like You. But they are altogether dull-hearted and foolish; a wooden idol is a worthless doctrine" (Jer. 10:6-8).

If your identity and security is in Christ, you will experience great freedom; but the very moment you prioritize something or someone above your Maker, and fail to see yourself as He has made you, you fall into the trap of idolatry. You set aside your eternal God in order to find temporary pleasure.

What is keeping you from walking in your true identity? It is so crucial to recognize the masks, or idols, that keep you from discovering who you were created to be. What follows are descriptions of false identities to which we often fall prey. Ask yourself which identities sound familiar in your life. You may want to circle or highlight the idols that are characteristic of you. Be honest. This is part of the journey to discover the true you.

Roller-Coaster Rhonda

Idol: Relationships
Misconception: Who I am in relationship with
determines who I am.
Truth: Matthew 10:37-39

Roller-Coaster Rhonda has based her identity in her relationship with her boyfriend. She is not a free spirit, but goes only where her boyfriend takes her. She will go to any length to please him. She often compromises sexually and seeks to give her boyfriend anything he wants. She often feels that if she can please him sexually, then she can always be in a relationship with him. She is overly dependent on him and has a difficult time making decisions unless he is right there by her side to make the decision for her. Whenever he is not around, she feels lost and lonely. She is always happy when he is right by her side, even though they may be having an argument. She will go to any length to see him and be with him. She believes that without him she is nothing, and she could not live or take one breath without his love.

Roller-Coaster Rhonda tends to be very clingy and insecure. If it were up to her, she would be in her boyfriend's presence all the time. Only around him does she feel complete and secure. She has a sense of belonging when she is wrapped in his arms and is the center of his attention and affection. Her day is good only if her boyfriend spends time with her and they are able to see each other. When they are not able to spend time together, she gets depressed and even fearful that something will happen to him or her. She prefers going along with whatever he says, at all times.

If Rhonda and her boyfriend were ever to break up, she would be a complete basket case with no idea of how to function or what to do with her time. She would feel completely devastated without him until another guy came along. Roller-Coaster Rhonda would then repeat the same cycle of gaining her security in her new boyfriend. In fact, she feels that if she is not in a relationship, something must be wrong with her.

What's wrong with being a Roller-coaster Rhonda? A relationship is not bad; but when it takes center stage over Christ, it becomes an idol. Roller-Coaster Rhonda looks to her boyfriend for security rather than to Christ. When we put any person ahead of Christ in our lives, we begin to worship that person instead of our Creator God. It doesn't matter whether this is a boyfriend, fiancé, husband, father or mother, son or daughter; our focus should always be on loving Christ supremely and finding our identity and security in Him. Jesus says in Mark 12:30, "'You shall love the LORD your God with all your heart, with all your soul, with all your mind, and with all your strength.' This is the first commandment."

Jesus' words recorded in Matthew 10:37-39 emphasize the importance of loving God more than any other human relationship: "He who loves father or mother more than Me is not worthy of Me. And he who loves son or daughter more than Me is not worthy of Me. And he who does not take his cross and follow after Me is not worthy of me. He who finds his life will lose it, and he who loses his life for My sake will find it." Jesus was not saying we should not have any other relationships or value our friendships, but that no human relationship should claim more of our love and attention than Christ.

Scripture also teaches that we are to flee from sexual immorality. Roller-Coaster Rhonda has failed to see God's best for her life as she compromises sexually with her boyfriend. Paul tells us in 1 Corinthians 6:15-20 that when a believer is joined with someone sexually, apart from marriage, she literally becomes as a prostitute:

> Do you not know that your bodies are members of Christ? Shall I then take the members of Christ and make them members of a harlot? Certainly not! Or do you not know that he who is joined to a harlot is one body with her? For "the two," He says, "shall become one flesh." But he who is joined to the Lord is one spirit with Him. Flee sexual immorality. Every sin that a man does is outside the body, but he who commits sexual immorality sins against his own body. Or do you not know that your body is the temple of the Holy Spirit who is in you, whom you have from God, and you are not your own? For you were bought at a price; therefore glorify God in your body and in your spirit, which are God's.

Roller-Coaster Rhonda's image of Christ is distorted due to the idolatry in her life. There will be no way for her to see how valuable she is to God or obtain her identity and security in Christ until she realizes the relationship idol in her life and surrenders it to the Lord. He longs for her to walk in her true identity and see how precious she is to Him.

Are you a Roller-Coaster Rhonda? If so, remember Matthew 6:24: "No one can serve two masters; for either he will hate the one and love the other, or else he will be loyal to the one and despise the other. You cannot serve God and mammon."

Monica Rose Brennan · www.regalbooks.com

Camouflage Cara

Idol: Acceptance/Pleasing People
Misconception: Who I hang out with determines who I am.
Truth: James 1:6-8; Galatians 1:6-8

Camouflage Cara blends in well with whatever environment she is in. She will do whatever is asked of her. She hates confrontation and prefers being at peace with everyone. Her way of being a peacemaker is simply to accept what everyone says and does. She goes along with any and all beliefs because she doesn't want to offend anyone. Her driving need is to be accepted by others regardless of who they are or what they are doing.

When she is at a party, she will do anything to be accepted. When she is at church, she will pretend to be like the people there in order to be accepted. She is double-minded and has forgotten her true identity. Without everyone's acceptance, she feels very insecure. She prefers blending in with the crowd and not being noticed especially. She longs for lasting friendships and desires only to please.

What's wrong with being a Camouflage Cara? Although a Camouflage Cara can make a great friend, she has no backbone of her own. She goes back and forth in her attempts to please others more than God. In her attempts to get the approval of others, she has forgotten that God accepts her as she is. James 1:6-8 speaks on the double-minded person: "For he who doubts is like a wave of the sea driven and tossed by the wind. For let not that man suppose that he will receive anything from the Lord; he is a double-minded man, unstable in all his ways." This passage is referring to walking by faith in the midst of difficult times; but it can also be applied to the woman who forgets who her Maker is and who she is. Whenever a person forgets her true identity, she begins to live a very unstable life.

Camouflage Cara may be blending in well with her different environments, but deep inside she is horribly discontent. The idol of acceptance is not lasting, because only true acceptance comes from Christ. The apostle Paul refers to pleasing others versus pleasing God: "I marvel that you are turning away so soon from him who called you in the grace of Christ, to a different gospel, which is not another; but there are some who trouble you and want to pervert the gospel of Christ. But even if we, or an angel from heaven, preach any other gospel to you than what you have received, let him be accursed. . . . For do I now persuade men, or God? Or do I seek to please men? For if I still pleased men, I would not be a bondservant of Christ" (Gal. 1:6-8,10). When we seek to please others more than Christ, we are practicing idolatry.

Are you a Camouflage Cara? If so, remember Matthew 6:24: "No one can serve two masters; for either he will hate the one and love the other, or else he will be loyal to the one and despise the other. You cannot serve God and mammon."

Plastic Patti

Idol: Body Image
Misconception: What I look like determines who I am.
Truth: 1 Peter 3:3-4

Style and fashion are obsessions to a Plastic Patti. Her identity is based solely on her outward appearance. Plastic Patti is always very concerned with what she is wearing and if she meets the popular opinions of society and culture. Hollywood is her guidebook. She is always aware of the latest fashions and latest products for her hair, face, nails and toes. She dresses to impress and feels that she must always be put together before anyone can see her.

She judges others using the same criteria. If she sees someone who is wearing something that doesn't measure up to the latest fashion, she makes sure she communicates it to someone else and, at times, even to the person. She may not verbally communicate with the person, but she communicates through her body language that the other person is inferior to her. Deep down, she feels very insecure. She tries to cover up her insecurities with makeup and clothes in order to gain the attention, admiration and love of others.

What's wrong with being a Plastic Patti? There is nothing wrong with looking nice, wearing nice clothes or makeup. But when these things are given greater priority than Christ, they become an idol. Instead of seeing herself as beautiful in God's eyes, Plastic Patti goes to the extreme and allows what she looks like to give her a sense of identity and worth. We are reminded of what true beauty is in 1 Peter 3:3-4: "Do not let your adornment be merely outward—arranging the hair, wearing gold, or putting on fine apparel—rather let it be the hidden person of the heart, with the incorruptible beauty of a gentle and quiet spirit, which is very precious in the sight of God."

Are you a Plastic Patti? If so, remember Matthew 6:24: "No one can serve two masters; for either he will hate the one and love the other, or else he will be loyal to the one and despise the other. You cannot serve God and mammon."

Frazzled Francis

Idol: Intelligence/Education
Misconception: How much I know determines
who I am and who I will become.
Truth: 1 Corinthians 2:9-13; 3:18-23

Frazzled Francis is a high achiever. She gains her significance through how much she knows about a particular subject. It is her number-one effort to be a straight-A student and the best academically in every area of achievement. She feels that when others do not join in this same passion, they are wasting their time pursuing other interests. She has no time for developing friendships or extracurricular activities. She has the future in her mind at all times and desires to be at the top in all of her endeavors.

When she experiences success, she feels significant and important. When she receives any grade lower than an A, she immediately believes it is someone else's error, never her own. She battles with pride. She doesn't like anyone to be ahead of her. She has no time for pointless conversations, and even small talk annoys her. Her greatest struggles are worry and anxiety. If she doesn't do well educationally, she believes she will not be hired in the position she has worked her hardest to gain. Although a high achiever, deep down she doesn't feel like she measures up. She has an obsessive fear of failure. This fear is what drives her to succeed. Her identity and security are tied to being the smartest and most likely to succeed.

What's wrong with being a Frazzled Francis? There is nothing wrong with desiring to succeed academically or intellectually. However, if you do not feel like you are anything when you are not the top of the list, then your identity has shifted from Christ to an idol. Paul writes that God's wisdom is greater than man's wisdom:

> But as it is written: "Eye has not seen, nor ear heard, nor have entered into the heart of man the things which God has prepared for those who love Him." But God has revealed them to us through His Spirit. For the Spirit searches all things, yes, the deep things of God. For what man knows the things of a man except the spirit of the man which is in him? Even so no one knows the things of God except the Spirit of God. Now we have received, not the spirit of the world, but the Spirit who is from God, that we might know the things that have been freely given to us by God. These things we also speak, not in words which man's wisdom teaches but which the Holy Spirit teaches, comparing spiritual things with spiritual (1 Cor. 2:9-13).

Frazzled Francis often boasts in her knowledge, but Paul reminds us that all boasting should be in Christ and Christ alone:

> Let no one deceive himself. If anyone among you seems to be wise in this age, let him become a fool that he may become wise. For the wisdom of this world is foolishness with God. For it is written, "He catches the wise in their own craftiness"; and again, "The LORD knows the thoughts

of the wise, that they are futile." Therefore let no one boast in men. For all things are yours: whether Paul or Apollos or Cephas, or the world or life or death, or things present or things to come—all are yours. And you are Christ's, and Christ is God's (1 Cor. 3:18-23).

Are you a Frazzled Francis? If so, remember Matthew 6:24: "No one can serve two masters; for either he will hate the one and love the other, or else he will be loyal to the one and despise the other. You cannot serve God and mammon."

Stressed-Out Sarah

Idol: Occupation/Profession/Career
Misconception: What I do for a living will determine who I am.
Truth: Philippians 3:1-10

Stressed-Out Sarah is consumed with her professional work. She thinks about it constantly, talks to others about it and even dreams about it. Her occupation and career are never off her mind. What she does is most definitely who she is. Without her job, she believes she would be nobody.

Stressed-Out Sarah has a 5-year calendar and has even mapped out her entire life for the next 10 years! She makes every effort to control everything that happens. She hates being behind on any information or unaware of last-minute changes to plans. She likes to know exactly what is expected from her and she wants to know this ahead of time so she can put forth her best effort. She dislikes anything last-minute or anything that is not for certain. She is obsessed with always having an objective and a plan of action in everything.

She is excellent at what she does, and employers constantly seek her out because she always puts her career first. However, she battles so much with success in her career that she feels constantly stressed. She worries a lot about circumstances that could possibly occur that are outside of her control. She fears that something will happen that would cause her to no longer have a career. She is usually not open to the advice of others when they have a plan for her that doesn't connect with a career. She has put her occupation ahead of her family and friends. She possesses a sense of significance when others associate her with her career and the excellent job she does.

Deep down, she still hasn't felt total contentment, but she believes that if she adds more objectives or goals to her calendar, it will fill her void. She experiences anxiety on a daily basis due to her desire to control her plans and her fears of not achieving them. Stressed-Out Sarah also has a difficult time trusting others to follow through. She feels that she is the best at what she does, so it is difficult for her to delegate anything. Those under her are micromanaged and are never given an opportunity to succeed, because she wants to make sure everything is done correctly.

What's wrong with being a Stressed-Out Sarah? There is nothing wrong with having a career or being successful. However, when these things make up a person's sole identity, they become an idol. If something were to happen to Stressed-Out Sarah's career, she would feel purposeless. She has forgotten that the Lord would take care of her. Sarah's eyes have wandered off of Christ and onto having her identity and security in her profession. Stressed-Out Sarah believes that she has no meaning in life without her profession.

Scripture reminds us of the importance of having confidence in Christ and not in ourselves. The apostle Paul wrote that being found in Christ (having your identity in Christ alone) is worth more than anything else the world could ever offer:

> But what things were gain to me, these I have counted loss for Christ. Yet indeed I also count all things loss for the excellence of the knowledge of Christ Jesus my Lord, for whom I have suffered the loss of all things, and count them as rubbish, that I may gain Christ and be found in Him, not having my own righteousness, which is from the law, but that which is through faith in Christ, the righteousness which is from God by faith; that I may know

Him and the power of His resurrection, and the fellowship of His sufferings, being conformed to His death, if, by any means, I may attain to the resurrection from the dead (Phil. 3:2-11).

Stressed-Out Sarah desperately needs to be reminded that being found in Christ is the greatest treasure, and everything else is nothing compared to Christ.

Are you a Stressed-Out Sarah? If so, remember Matthew 6:24: "No one can serve two masters; for either he will hate the one and love the other, or else he will be loyal to the one and despise the other. You cannot serve God and mammon."

Wasteful Wilma

Idol: Money
Misconception: How much I have will determine who I am.
Truth: Luke 15:11-32

Money is the name of the game for Wasteful Wilma. Her material possessions are the most important treasures in her life. She is driven to look the best and have the best. She believes that money is the answer to her identity and security. She is on a continual cycle to gain more. She bases her self-worth on how much she possesses. Wasteful Wilma believes that if she has more money and things, she will have more of everything else, including acceptance and friends. Without money, she would not be able to survive because money is her life.

Wasteful Wilma's greatest stress reliever is spending money. She believes her day has been wasted if she hasn't purchased something. She has a desire to buy things that she doesn't need and sometimes goes to any lengths to purchase something she likes, even if she cannot afford it. She has many credit cards and isn't always the best manager of her money. People enjoy being around Wasteful Wilma because she likes to have a lot of fun and purchase fun things for others to gain their acceptance. Deep down, she longs to belong to something and to feel secure. She believes that if she is wealthy, she will conquer these desires.

What's wrong with being a Wasteful Wilma? There is nothing wrong with having money or even a lot of money; however, if you put money ahead of Christ, you practice idolatry. Paul reminds us of the importance of practicing contentment—of being satisfied with what we have been given:

> Now godliness with contentment is great gain. For we brought nothing into this world, and it is certain we can carry nothing out. And having food and clothing, with these we shall be content. But those who desire to be rich fall into temptation and a snare, and into many foolish and harmful lusts which drown men in destruction and perdition. For the love of money is a root of all kinds of evil, for which some have strayed from the faith in their greediness, and pierced themselves through with many sorrows (1 Tim. 6:6-10).

The desire for more can overtake anyone when their focus shifts from Christ. Verse 10 reminds us that some believers have even "strayed from the faith" because of their love of money.

Do you remember the story of the prodigal son found in Luke 15:11-32? It is an excellent example of someone who forgot his identity, turning from his father in order to focus on the fleeting pleasures of the world. The prodigal son placed material possessions and pleasure as the number-one priority in his life. His father gave him his inheritance early when the son requested it; the son wasted it all and was left with nothing.

Although the son fell into idolatry, his father waited for him to return home. The son repented, and the father immediately forgave him. Our heavenly Father does the same with us. Even though we may go through seasons where we waste our life, He receives us back into His arms and forgives us when we repent and turn toward Him. Wasteful Wilma needs to be reminded that only Christ, not money, gives her identity.

Are you a *Wasteful Wilma*? If so, remember Matthew 6:24: "No one can serve two masters; for either he will hate the one and love the other, or else he will be loyal to the one and despise the other. You cannot serve God and mammon."

Duty-Driven Debra

Idol: Religious Works
Misconception: Religious works determine who I am.
Truth: Matthew 6:1-4; 7:21-23

Duty-Driven Debra feels a sense of obligation to do things just because they need to be done. She has a deep-rooted desire to help others but gains her sense of significance on her good works. She is usually the first to volunteer to help and serve in the church. She feels like she needs to be the first to arrive at a church function and the last to leave, even though there are others there to help. She is kind-hearted, dependable and trustworthy; however, she does things more out of a sense of duty than joy. She has lost her focus, just like Martha of Bethany (see Luke 10:38-42). She often complains if others are not helping. However, when others try to help, she is the first to criticize them for not doing it the correct way. She has lost sight of the most important thing: loving God.

Deep down, she feels no gladness. She enjoys a sense of pride when she does something good for others. She gains her sense of significance the most by being recognized for all she has done for the church and community. If she isn't noticed, it bothers her. She desires desperately to please others. She believes the more good works she does, the better Christian she is. However, Duty-Driven Debra doesn't remember the last time she read her Bible or had a prayer time in private. She knows something is missing in her life, but what is it?

What's wrong with being a Duty-Driven Debra? A Duty-Driven Debra is so appreciated by the church and community because of her desire to help. There is nothing wrong with doing good things. In fact, practicing good works is a commendable service. Scripture calls us to do good works. However, if what we do is based on a sense of obligation or because we want to be recognized by others, we have lost our focus. As Jesus said:

> Take heed that you do not do your charitable deeds before men, to be seen by them. Otherwise you have no reward from your Father in heaven. Therefore, when you do a charitable deed, do not sound a trumpet before you as the hypocrites do in the synagogues and in the streets, that they may have glory from men. Assuredly, I say to you, they have their reward. But when you do a charitable deed, do not let your left hand know what your right hand is doing, that your charitable deed may be in secret; and your Father who sees in secret will Himself reward you openly (Matt. 6:1-4).

True good works will bring glory to Christ. In Matthew 7:21-23, Jesus reminds us that we can be doing things in His name and even portray to others that we are following Him, but if we haven't experienced a true relationship with Him, we have lost our focus completely: "Not everyone who says to Me, 'Lord, Lord,' shall enter the kingdom of heaven, but he who does the will of My Father in heaven. Many will say to Me in that day, 'Lord, Lord, have we not prophesied in Your name, cast out demons in Your name, and done many wonders in Your name?' And then I will declare to them, 'I never knew you; depart from Me, you who practice lawlessness!'"

Duty-Driven Debra needs to be reminded that true joy comes only when she is gaining her strength and sense of significance in Christ, not by practicing good works out of obligation or to be applauded.

Are you a Duty-Driven Debra? If so, remember Matthew 6:24: "No one can serve two masters; for either he will hate the one and love the other, or else he will be loyal to the one and despise the other. You cannot serve God and mammon."

Entertainer Evelyn

Idol: Hobbies/Interests
Misconception: What I choose to do determines who I am.
Truth: Matthew 4:18-22

Entertainer Evelyn is driven by a need to entertain herself with what she chooses to like. She is consumed with her latest interest. Although that interest may change from time to time, or stay the same, she is solely identified by her hobby or interest. Without it, she believes she would have no reason to live. The sport or hobby she is engaged in always comes first. She absolutely loves embracing everything about this interest. Anyone who knows her associates her with this sport or hobby, because she is constantly talking about it. Others like to be around Entertainer Evelyn because she is a lot of fun and enjoys what she does. She often brings on the attention of others without even realizing it.

If anything were to happen to her physically so that she could not engage in this activity, she doesn't know what she would do. Entertainer Evelyn dislikes spare time. She finds it necessary to always have something going on. When she has spare time, she is forced to think about serious matters. Deep down, she longs to be still and quiet and know who she really is, but she has lost focus of her identity in Christ and has replaced it with her personal interests. She no longer has time to spend with Christ, reading the Bible or praying.

What's wrong with being an Entertainer Evelyn? There is nothing wrong with sports, entertainment, hobbies or other interests. However, an interest of this kind can easily become an idol. Two of Jesus' disciples enjoyed fishing. One day, as Jesus was walking, He called to them and asked them to follow Him. Without hesitation, Peter and Andrew left their nets to follow Jesus. Although Peter and

Andrew enjoyed fishing, and it was their livelihood, they were not controlled by it. Following Christ was more important to them.

Jesus, walking by the Sea of Galilee, saw two brothers, Simon called Peter, and Andrew his brother, casting a net into the sea; for they were fishermen. Then He said to them, "Follow Me, and I will make you fishers of men." They immediately left their nets and followed Him. Going on from there, He saw two other brothers, James the son of Zebedee, and John his brother, in the boat with Zebedee their father, mending their nets. He called them, and immediately they left the boat and their father, and followed Him (Matt. 4:18-22).

Entertainer Evelyn needs to be reminded that following Christ is the most important thing, not a sport or hobby.

Are you an Entertainer Evelyn? If so, remember Matthew 6:24: "No one can serve two masters; for either he will hate the one and love the other, or else he will be loyal to the one and despise the other. You cannot serve God and mammon."

Backward Betsy

Idol: The Past
Misconception: My history determines who I am.
Truth: Philippians 3:12-14

Backward Betsy cannot ever seem to forget her past. She spends a lot of her time in condemnation over past failures and sins. She cannot seem to grasp the fact that she is forgiven. She can never seem to move forward because she keeps clinging to the past. She identifies herself solely on the sins she has committed and believes others see her that way as well. Whenever she shares her testimony, it is always about her past and never on what God is doing in her life now. She longs to forgive herself, but at the same time she believes her past will always define her. She gains her significance based on the pity she receives from others. Backward Betsy has forgotten her true identity in Christ. She has started to flirt with the same things she once was delivered from. She longs to experience freedom but she believes she will never experience true victory, so she continues in the sins of her past.

What's wrong with being a Backward Betsy? It is good to remember where God has brought you from; but when you gain your sole identity based on your past, and when you go back to the things that once held you captive, you practice idolatry.

Backward Betsy needs to be reminded that God loves her and forgives her: "As far as the east is from the west, so far has He removed our transgressions from us" (Ps. 103:12). True freedom will come to Backward Betsy only when she stops flirting with the past and turns back to Christ. Paul reminds us in Philippians 3:12-14 to forget the past and reach toward Christ: "Not that I have already attained, or am already perfected; but I press on, that I may lay hold of that for which Christ Jesus has also laid hold of me. Brethren, I do not count myself to have apprehended; but one thing I do, forgetting those things which are behind and reaching forward to those things which are ahead, I press toward the goal for the prize of the upward call of God in Christ Jesus."

Are you a Backward Betsy? If so, remember Matthew 6:24: "No one can serve two masters; for either he will hate the one and love the other, or else he will be loyal to the one and despise the other. You cannot serve God and mammon."

Spotlight Susan

Idol: Attention of Others
Misconception: My ability to get others to notice
me determines who I am.
Truth: Galatians 1:6-10

Spotlight Susan is driven to gain the attention of others. She is most fulfilled and gratified when she is the center of attention, and she will go to great lengths to get others to notice her. She feels accepted when she makes others laugh. Spotlight Susan loves to be admired, and she justifies the drama by saying it is just her personality. She gets her energy from being around people, and people love being around her because she is a lot of fun.

She is kindhearted and personifies a happy-go-lucky personality. However, without others' glamorous opinions of her, she feels shattered inside and feels as if no one cares. She has an insatiable desire to be loved and honestly believes that if someone is giving her attention of any kind it means they love her. The desire for center stage affects every area of her life, from her wardrobe to her speech. She is a natural influencer of others because she makes others believe that she is not afraid of people, and she will go to any lengths to get their attention or praise. Deep down, Spotlight Susan longs for acceptance and true friendship. She is terrified that others will not like her.

What's wrong with being a Spotlight Susan? There is nothing wrong with the desire to please others, make friends or bring them laughter. However, when it becomes a person's sole identity instead of gaining significance from Christ, it becomes an idol. In Galatians 1:10, Paul reminds us that we should be seeking to please only Christ: "For do I now persuade men, or God? Or do I seek to please men? For if I still pleased men, I would not be a bondservant of Christ."

Are you a Spotlight Susan? Remember Matthew 6:24: "No one can serve two masters; for either he will hate the one and love the other, or else he will be loyal to the one and despise the other. You cannot serve God and mammon."

Hurt Hannah

Idol: Sickness, Pain
Misconception: My current troubles determine who I am.
Truth: Galatians 1:6-10

Hurt Hannah bases her identity on her current troubles. She experiences a lot of sickness and pain from day to day—sometimes physically and sometimes emotionally. Instead of trusting in Christ to strengthen her, she complains about her hurts. She has allowed her physical discomforts, disabilities and/or handicaps to define her. She longs to be accepted by others but feels that in order to get people to recognize her she must tell them about all the many ways she has been hurt or the sickness she is experiencing. She struggles with bitterness and the unfairness of life. She doesn't understand why she must suffer when others do not. However, without her sickness, she is not sure who she would be, because she has allowed it to take over her life instead of Christ.

What's wrong with being a Hurt Hannah? There are many people who suffer with different types of pain and disabilities. It's not bad to voice your hurts and discomforts; but when they become your identity other than Christ, then focusing on your hurts becomes an idol.

The woman with the issue of blood, whose story is recorded in Mark 5:25-34, had major health problems for more than 12 years! Long story short: Jesus healed her and called her His daughter! In the last part of this passage, He says, "Daughter, your faith has made you well. Go in peace, and be healed of your affliction" (v. 34). The woman could have kept identifying herself as a woman of sickness in order to gain the attention of others, but instead she walked in her newfound identity.

Are you a Hurt Hannah? If so, remember Matthew 6:24: "No one can serve two masters; for either he will hate the one and love the other, or else he will be loyal to the one and despise the other. You cannot serve God and mammon."

Recognizing the Danger of Idolatry

Within the heart of every woman is the desire and need to be identified—to know who we and Whose we are. However, we so often allow temporal things—relationships, people, body image, education, career, money, religion or hobbies—to become our main means of identity. These things are not wrong in and of themselves; but when they become the reason we live, we not only begin wearing a mask, but we also begin living a lifestyle of masquerade rather than a lifestyle of identity.

Would you say that you are living a life of true idolatry or true identity? As you learned earlier in this book, you first discover who you are by asking your Maker and Designer, Jesus Christ, to come into your life. As you ask Christ to come into your life, you are not only recognizing your need for Him, but you are also confessing and repenting of your sins. He has promised to forgive you of your sins, regardless of the offense, and to come and live in you when you ask Him in true faith. This is the first step in discovering who you are.

However, after we have our true identity in Christ, we often enter into deception, like Eve, and we forget the freedom, peace, contentment and joy we have in Christ, and we begin to think that we are in want. Before we know it, we pick up the mask we had on before we became His daughter.

The amazing thing about our Creator is that He is a God of grace. If we realize the mess we are in, He is always ready to clean us up and give us a second chance, just as He gave Adam and Eve a second chance.

Are you ready to get rid of the idols in your life? It is so important to recognize these idols and ask Christ to forgive you for putting them in first place, and then repent of your sins and come back to the Father, just as the prodigal son did. He is waiting for you with open arms, and He longs to have intimate fellowship with you again.

Dear God,
Forgive me for the idols I have had in my life that have kept me back from placing You as number one in my life. May You have all of my attention and devotion. Help me to be captivated more by You than the temporary pleasures of the world. Give me Your strength to walk in my true identity instead of true idolatry.
In Your name I pray, amen.

YOUR PRAYER

_____
_____
_____
_____
_____
_____
_____
_____
_____
_____

WHAT DO YOU THINK?

Describe a time when you were tempted to turn away from your
devotion to Christ and go to something else you thought you
needed more.

_____
_____
_____
_____

What is the truth found in Psalm 139 that assures you of how
much God loves you?

_____
_____
_____
_____

Why is it important to identify specific idols that may be present in your life as a believer?

_____

_____

_____

_____

_____

_____

Is there anything wrong with being in a relationship, having a hobby or an interest? Why or why not?

_____

_____

_____

_____

_____

_____

Name the idol you believe you struggle with as described in this chapter. How do you think this idol has been a hindrance to your true identity?

_____

_____

_____

_____

_____

_____

How does Psalm 135:15-18 describe an idol?

_____

_____

_____

_____

_____

_____

What is the danger in worshiping something or someone other than Christ?

_____

_____

_____

_____

_____

What must you do to get rid of the idols in your life?

_____

_____

_____

_____

_____

Unchanging Truths to Read and Treasure

LEVITICUS 19:4
MATTHEW 4:18-22; 6:1-4; 7:21-23; 10:37-39
LUKE 15:11-32
1 CORINTHIANS 2:9-13; 3:18-23
2 CORINTHIANS 11:3-4
GALATIANS 1:6-10
PHILIPPIANS 3:1-10,12-14
JAMES 1:6-8
1 PETER 3:3-4
1 JOHN 5:20-21

SECTION THREE

Imagery Reflected

For it is the God who commanded light to shine out of darkness, who has shone in our hearts to give the light of the knowledge of the glory of God in the face of Jesus Christ.
2 CORINTHIANS 4:6

The fact that I am a woman does not make me a different kind of Christian, but the fact that I am a Christian does make me a different kind of woman.
ELISABETH ELLIOT, *LET ME BE A WOMAN*

My prayer for each of you is that you labor in the work from the rising of the morning till the stars appear (Nehemiah 4:21): that is, from your earliest days, the days of your morning, till the last days, the days of your evening, when He whom not seeing you love will call you home to see His face.
AMY CARMICHAEL, *CANDLES IN THE DARK*

CHAPTER SEVEN

More Than Meets the Eye

Secrets to Remaining Steadfast in Your Commitment to Live out Your Identity Unmasked

Therefore we do not lose heart. Even though our outward man is perishing, yet the inward man is being renewed day by day. For our light affliction, which is but for a moment, is working for us a far more exceeding and eternal weight of glory, while we do not look at the things which are seen, but at the things which are not seen. For the things which are seen are temporary, but the things which are not seen are eternal.

2 CORINTHIANS 4:16-18

Do not let your adornment be merely outward—arranging the hair, wearing gold, or putting on fine apparel—rather let it be the hidden person of the heart, with the incorruptible beauty of a gentle and quiet spirit, which is very precious in the sight of God.

1 PETER 3:3-4

My eyes studied her beautiful smile, blue eyes, perfectly arched eyebrows and shining black hair. I thought that even her nose was perfect. If I could only look like her, I would be so happy.

My mother's nose was slightly pointed and a picture of perfection to my 10-year-old eyes. My nose was simply round at the tip, with no point at all. If my nose were slightly pointed, most assuredly my face would seem slimmer than it appeared. Why did I get stuck with my father's nose, and not my mother's nose? There had to be a way to look more like my mother.

Day and night I began to gently rub my nose in a downward position, pinching it at the end. Hopefully, this action would cause my nose to become different than it was. The only results from this repetitive procedure were a tired hand and a nose that was now blistered red.

Did you ever want to be just like your mother when you grew up? Or perhaps you wished you resembled someone else that you admired? I went to great lengths to be like the person I admired the most. When my mother would do her hair a certain way, that is the way I would want to do my hair. If she wore a red shirt, I would wear a red shirt. Wherever she went, I followed her. I was her shadow, and I made it my aim to go everywhere she went.

Before long, people said how much I was like my mother. These comments were huge compliments to me, because I esteemed her so much and wanted to be as much like her as possible. I loved my mother very much, and I still do.

A Striking Resemblance

We were made in the likeness of Christ. If we have chosen to follow Him, we have been given a new name and a true identity. We literally have become a new creature (see 2 Cor. 5:17). As we live out our new name and true identity, we no longer live for ourselves, but for our Maker. We live out our identity in Him by walking with Him—spending time with Him, talking to Him, reading His Word.

When I first placed my faith in Christ. I remember that I couldn't get enough of learning about God, my marvelous Maker. It is still that way for me. He has become everything to me!

Remember this verse? "So God created man in His own image; in the image of God He created him; male and female He created them" (Gen. 1:27). It's so easy to become mesmerized with the outward appearance, or image, of someone; but the focus in this verse is the soul. Our Maker has no outward image that we were created to resemble, but rather inward characteristics that should be found in all of His creation as they live out their true identity. You and I were made in His image, in His likeness, for the purpose of resembling Him . . . taking after His character. The more time we spend with Him, living out our true identity, the more we resemble Him.

One of the most beautiful women I had the privilege to spend time with was a widowed woman named Annie. Annie was in her 80s and was known by everyone as a godly woman. She was the picture of someone who is filled with the aroma of Christ: "Now thanks be to God who always leads us in triumph in Christ, and through us diffuses the fragrance of His knowledge in every place. For we are to God the fragrance of Christ among those who are being saved and among those who are perishing" (2 Cor. 2:14-15). Annie definitely had the fragrance of Christ.

There was something remarkably different about Annie compared to many other women I had met. I have so many memories of her walking around to different people in the church, encouraging them and praying over them. When I went off to college, I would always try to visit her on my breaks.

During one break, I found out that she had cancer. However, Annie was still praising God! She made it her aim to tell everyone not to feel sorry for her, because her Maker was in control of everything. I remember the large globe of the world she would keep beside her chair in her small living room. She shared with me on one occasion that she would never be able to travel as a missionary to other regions of the world, but she could pray over different regions of the world. Every day she would pray for a different people group and their salvation. She most definitely was a missionary, even in her sickness.

One of the last memories I have of Annie is when I went over to her house and knocked on the door as I usually did. When I didn't hear anything, I started to worry, thinking perhaps something had happened to her. I called her name louder and began to knock harder. In a very quiet voice, I heard her call to me, "Over here, I am over here." I turned around, and there was Annie, sitting on the ground under a beautiful tree that was giving her shade in the hot sun. She was wearing a bonnet to protect her face.

I immediately went over to sit down beside her and told her how good it was to see her. Inside, I was thinking, *What is she doing out here in the hot sun, under a tree?*

I will never forget the first words out of her mouth. "Have you ever noticed how many different shades of green there are?"

How many different shades of green? Was she serious? What was she talking about? Inside, I was thinking, *No, I honestly haven't ever noticed.* I didn't realize it at that moment, but Annie was still teaching me about our Maker. She had such a sense of wonder about God, and she was still marveling at His creation after living a long life.

Annie resembled her Maker more than anyone I know. Although her face was wrinkled, her hair thinning, and she could barely walk without extreme pain, she was one of the most beautiful women I have ever met. She resembled her God. She had a different kind of beauty—a beauty I wanted to possess and imitate. I wanted to be like her because she was like Christ. Remember what the apostle Paul said in 1 Corinthians 11:1? He said, "Imitate me, just as I also imitate Christ." Although Annie never vocalized those exact words to me, her actions shouted, "Monica, imitate me, just as I also imitate Christ!"

Something Is Different About You!

The beauty Annie possessed is the same radiance we are called to walk in as God's peculiar (chosen and special) women. Peter calls this beauty "incorruptible," and he gives us a striking contrast between the focus of those who walk in their true identity and those who do not: "Do not let your adornment be merely outward—arranging the hair, wearing gold, or putting on fine apparel—rather let it be the hidden person of the heart, with the incorruptible beauty of a gentle and quiet spirit, which is very precious in the sight of God" (1 Pet. 3:3-4). Annie's attractiveness did not come from her outward appearance, but from the inward qualities that resembled her magnificent Creator. Yet, I fear that we spend so much time taking care of our outward shell that we leave little time to spend on our inward soul, which was made to reflect the glory and image of God.

Take It as a Compliment

Has anyone ever come up to you and said, "You're different"? Perhaps you made a decision not to go to a party that everyone else was going to, or you decided not to go out with a guy who was very attractive but not a Christian. Perhaps your husband hasn't been the spiritual leader you have wanted him to be, but you show him respect as 1 Peter 3:1-2 instructs, not necessarily because he deserves it but because you are going to trust in God and His Word.

Our actions make us different. When we truly follow Christ and walk in our true identity, we possess strength from our Maker to act as He would have us act. In 1 Peter 2:21-25, we are reminded of the one who is our prime example for living:

> For to this you were called, because Christ also suffered for us, leaving us an example, that you should follow His steps: "Who committed no sin, nor was deceit found in His mouth"; who, when He was reviled, did not revile in return; when He suffered, he did not threaten, but committed Himself to Him who judges righteously; who Himself bore our sins in His own body on the tree, that we, having died to sins, might live for righteousness—by whose stripes you were healed. For you were like sheep going

astray, but have now returned to the Shepherd and Over-
seer of your souls.

We were created to walk in the steps of Christ. This does not
mean that we were created to be perfect. We know that Christ was
the only human who never sinned. However, when we become a
new creation in Christ and begin to live out our true identity, we
become very *peculiar*. Has anyone ever called you "peculiar"? We
should take such statements as the highest compliment: "But you
are a chosen generation, a royal priesthood, a holy nation, His own
special people, that you may proclaim the praises of Him who
called you out of darkness into His marvelous light; who once were
not a people but are now the people of God, who had not obtained
mercy but now have obtained mercy" (1 Pet. 2:9-10).

Being peculiar (chosen, special) does not come from any ability of our own, but it occurs naturally as we are following Christ.
If we don't seem different from the world, then we are not walking
in our true identity.

It's Not Always Easy to Do
One of the first principles I learned in remaining steadfast in my
true identity was not to be ashamed of being different. In other
words, not to be ashamed of my Maker: "Beloved, I beg you as so-
journers and pilgrims, abstain from fleshly lusts which war against
the soul, having your conduct honorable among the Gentiles, that
when they speak against you as evildoers, they may, by your good
works which they observe, glorify God in the day of visitation"
(1 Pet. 2:11-12). When we live out our faith in Christ, those who do
not know Christ may be able to see Him in us and glorify Him one
day. Ask yourself, "Do I resemble my Maker?" When others observe you, do they see someone who is different?

It's difficult to be different sometimes, especially when we are
tempted to cave in to the world's influence in order to be accepted
by others. When I was a senior in high school, I played tennis and
became a member of the Fellowship of Christian Athletes. Anyone

could attend this club, even if he or she was not actively involved in sports. However, I thought it would be good to offer another club that didn't focus only on sports.

I was able to find a teacher who agreed to be a sponsor, and I began a Christian club on my public school campus. I really believed the Lord had put this on my heart. I didn't have any idea who would sign up or if anyone would show interest in the club. It was extremely rare to find anyone who proclaimed to be a Christian and lived out his or her faith in Christ. If you took any type of stand for Christ, you really did stick out, and at times you were made fun of for your faith. I realized that like never before when the day came for me to announce the new Christian club.

I named the club "First Priority." We stood for three principles: (1) drug free, (2) alcohol free, and (3) sexual abstinence before marriage. When club day came, I was so excited. I remember looking at my high school as the mission field God had given me to be His witness. I wanted so desperately to be His light at school and for my friends to place their faith in Christ. I got out my display and stood behind the table as my classmates began to wander around to the different clubs that interested them.

One of my friends came up to the display. When I started to say "Hey . . ." he began to openly mock me. He thought sexual abstinence before marriage was ridiculous and made sure he told me so. I remember turning blood red in the face and not knowing what to say.

In the moment when he began to ridicule me, I almost caved in. To tell you the truth, I wanted to cave in. I wanted to say, "You know, this is so stupid and totally not worth it." But then the verse of Scripture came to my mind from Romans 1:16: "For I am not ashamed of the gospel of Christ, for it is the power of God to salvation for everyone who believes, for the Jew first and also for the Greek." I had a choice in that moment: Was I going to be ashamed of the gospel, or was I willing to look different, strange, peculiar? I began to pray silently, "Lord, I will not be ashamed of Your gospel; give me Your strength to stand."

A Moment-by-Moment Surrender

As you make a commitment to remain steadfast in living out your true identity, you are making a commitment to be His peculiar woman. The more time you spend with your Maker, the more you will resemble Him and the more strength He will give you to stand for truth in the midst of a culture that is so deceived. Surrender is a daily process as you ask Him for strength to stand and not be ashamed of His gospel.

We are called to be peculiar in every aspect of our lifestyle and every part of us—our eyes, ears, hands, feet, minds, emotions, dress, walk and talk. When we say we are a follower of Jesus Christ, we can expect ridicule and persecution. It is in those moments when our faith is not only tested, but we also have an opportunity to resemble our Lord and point others to Him.

I love to look at old family pictures, especially around Christmas time. My mother usually gets out pictures from previous Christmas gatherings and puts them on the refrigerator for our family and friends to look at. The other day, I noticed several pictures of me on the refrigerator door. Honestly, I didn't like the majority of them! Have you ever liked the way you looked in every picture ever taken of you? I sure haven't; I've wanted to tear some of them up!

If God were to take a picture of our inward attributes—what God has created to reflect Him—what would we want to do with the pictures once we saw them? Would we be ashamed? Would we want to tear them up so no one could ever see them? A lot of us can put on a good show in front of others. Only God knows if we are really living out our true identity.

In 1 Corinthians 3, Paul tells us that we are the temple of God and that all of our works will be tested to reveal our true motives. Do we walk out our true identity by being His peculiar women regardless of the pressures in society to look like everybody else? Or do we cave in to the pressures of the world and pretend to be His peculiar women whenever it is convenient and nonthreatening?

For we are God's fellow workers; you are God's field, you are God's building. According to the grace of God which was given to me, as a wise master builder I have laid the foundation, and another builds on it. But let each one take heed how he builds on it. For no other foundation can anyone lay than that which is laid, which is Jesus Christ. Now if anyone builds on this foundation with gold, silver, precious stones, wood, hay, straw, each one's work will become clear; for the Day will declare it, because it will be revealed by fire; and the fire will test each one's work, of what sort it is. If anyone's work which he has built on it endures, he will receive a reward. If anyone's work is burned, he will suffer loss; but he himself will be saved, yet so as through fire. Do you not know that you are the temple of God and that the Spirit of God dwells in you? If anyone defiles the temple of God, God will destroy him. For the temple of God is holy, which temple you are (1 Cor. 3:9-17).

We are His holy and peculiar people, called to live out our true identity. How peculiar (set apart from the world's values) is your portrait?

What Keeps Us Steadfast

So what helps us remain committed to Christ? What gives us the strength we need to keep living out our true identity? It's critical that we read and study God's Word. As we make a faith commitment to follow Christ, we are also making a faith commitment to His Word.

In John 1:1-5, we learn that God is and always has been the Word. They are one and the same: "In the beginning was the Word, and the Word was with God, and the Word was God. He was in the beginning with God. All things were made through Him, and without Him nothing was made that was made. In Him was life, and the life was the light of men. And the light shines in the darkness, and the darkness did not comprehend it."

What God teaches us from the Scriptures will never contradict what He instructs us to do on a daily basis. For example, His Word instructs us not to be unequally yoked to an unbeliever (see 2 Cor. 6:14). Thus, He would never give you peace to date an unbeliever, because that would go against His Word, and God does not lie (see Num. 23:19; Titus 1:2), and He does not change (see Mal. 3:6).

To remain steadfast and live out our true identity we must see the value of the Scriptures. As we grow in our faith, we must see the importance and value of saturating ourselves with the truth of His Word on a daily basis. In them, we learn about our Maker and His marvelous plans and purposes for us. Again, the more time we spend in the Word and learn about our Creator, the more we will begin to resemble Him, thus becoming more and more peculiar.

He has promised to give us the strength we need to stand and to remain steadfast! But we must continually—daily—be reminded of the difference between God's image of us and the mold the world desires to place us in. God's truth will enable you to recognize the lies of our society and will help you to be all He has created you to be!

Qualities to Live For

Now let's break down our true identity even more by reflecting on all the different ways we are called to be peculiar. Remember, we are called to be holy as He is holy. What does it mean to be His holy and peculiar people? It simply means to be different from the world. As we spend time with Christ on a daily basis and grow in our walk with Him, there should be an obvious difference in our lifestyle versus the lifestyle of the world.

What We Look At

How peculiar are your eyes? Are they becoming mesmerized with the Truth from reading God's Word, or are they more focused on the images of the world? Remember, *Eve had trouble with her eyes*, didn't she? She took her eyes off of her Maker and began to see something she felt she lacked instead of embracing all that God had given her.

So often we spend our time looking at everything we think will please us instead of being content in Jesus. As we look to Him on a daily basis, He gives us the joy and strength to stand for Him and to watch for His return.

We read in 1 John 2:15, "Do not love the world or the things in the world. If anyone loves the world, the love of the Father is not in him. For all that is in the world—the lust of the flesh, the lust of the eyes, and the pride of life—is not of the Father but is of the world. And the world is passing away and the lust of it; but he who does the will of God abides forever." There is nothing lasting that the world can give us. The only eternal thing we can possess is our relationship with God.

Proverbs 17:24 reminds us of the wisdom from God versus the temporary things of the world: "Wisdom is in the sight of him who has understanding, but the eyes of a fool are on the ends of the earth." In what ways are we using our eyes for God's glory? Do we have eyes of compassion that see the needs of others? Are we using our eyes to read the Word of God and devotional books that help us grow in our faith? *Oh, that we would stop looking at the world and use our eyes for His glory.*

What We Listen To

How peculiar are your ears? I don't know about you, but I have wasted too much time in the past listening to lies: "You're not good enough." "You've blown it." "There is no hope for you." "It's not actually sin." "There is no harm in a little compromise."

Remember, *Eve had trouble with her ears,* didn't she? "You will be like God, knowing good and evil" (Gen. 3:5). Eve listened to lies rather than God's truth. Proverbs 18:15 reminds us of the importance of being wise with our ears: "The heart of the prudent acquires knowledge, and the ear of the wise seeks knowledge." *Oh, that we would stop listening to the Deceiver who is powerful in this present world and use our ears for God's glory.*

What We Say

How peculiar is your mouth? I wonder how much time we spend spreading gossip about other women? Instead of praying for one another, we talk behind one another's backs. Whether it is the truth or a lie, we have no business talking in a negative way about another person. What would happen if we would begin to pray for instead of slandering one another? *Eve had trouble with her mouth,* didn't she? She began to have a conversation with sin itself . . . with the serpent. James shows us the danger of the tongue and the mess it can create when our focus is not on Christ:

> Even so the tongue is a little member and boasts great things. See how great a forest a little fire kindles! And the tongue is a fire, a world of iniquity. The tongue is so set among our members that it defiles the whole body, and sets on fire the course of nature; and it is set on fire by hell. For every kind of beast and bird, of reptile and creature of the sea, is tamed and has been tamed by mankind. But no man can tame the tongue. It is an unruly evil, full of deadly poison. With it we bless our God and Father, and with it we curse men, who have been made in the similitude of God. Out of the same mouth proceed blessing and cursing. My brethren, these things ought not to be so. Does a spring send forth fresh water and bitter from the same opening? Can a fig tree, my brethren, bear olives, or a grapevine bear figs? Thus no spring yields both salt water and fresh (Jas. 3:5-12).

Wow! What a convicting passage. Take in what James is teaching in verse 12: If we say we have a new identity in Christ, then our tongue—the words we speak—should be different from the world's talk. Instead of gossiping about one another, we should be praying for one another. Instead of cursing one another, we should be blessing one another. *Oh, that we would use our mouths for God's glory.*

What We Do and Where We Go

How peculiar are your hands and feet? Do your hands reach out to those in need or do they selfishly cling to the temporary pleasures of the world? Do your hands reach out in love toward others or do they make a fist and make an enemy? Do your hands rise in praise to God to be seen by others or do they fold secretly in prayer and worship?

Where do your feet take you? Remember, *Eve had trouble with her hands and feet*, didn't she? She reached out and took of the fruit of the tree she was told would cause death. Her feet wandered in the wrong direction. How many times have our hands and feet gone in the opposite direction from the will of our Maker?

> If your hand or foot causes you to sin, cut it off and cast it from you. It is better for you to enter into life lame or maimed, rather than having two hands or two feet, to be cast into the everlasting fire. And if your eye causes you to sin, pluck it out and cast it from you. It is better for you to enter into life with one eye, rather than having two eyes, to be cast into hell fire (Matt. 18:8-9).

This Scripture passage isn't referring to actually cutting off your hands and feet, but to get rid of anything that is causing you not to live out your true identity in Christ. *Oh, that we would use our hands and feet only for God's glory.*

What We Think About

How peculiar is your mind? What do you spend most of your time and energies thinking about? Do you allow your mind to question God's design and plan for your life, or do you saturate your thoughts with truth? The apostle Paul encourages us to meditate on Christ:

> Finally, brethren, whatever things are true, whatever things are noble, whatever things are just, whatever things are

pure, whatever things are lovely, whatever things are of good report, if there is any virtue and if there is anything praise-worthy—meditate on these things. The things which you learned and received and heard and saw in me, these do, and the God of peace will be with you (Phil. 4:8-9).

What should we dwell on? Whatever is *true, noble, just, pure, lovely* and *of good report*. These are the characteristics of Christ Himself. We are instructed to turn our attention to Christ, who is the truth, and not to lies. *Eve had trouble with her mind,* didn't she? She opened up her mind to listen to the lies of the devil versus God's truth. As we meditate on God and His truth, we are promised that His peace will be with us. *Oh, that we would use our minds for His glory versus the world's.*

What Rules Our Responses

How peculiar are your emotions? Have you given your emotions over to God or do you feel controlled by them? Do you live your life driven by feelings, or by passion? Passion is not a feeling; it is a determination to remain steadfast in your commitment to live out your true identity.

Christ is our prime example of this in His death on the cross for our sins. He was not experiencing any warm and fuzzy feelings; rather, we see His passion to be obedient to the Father so that we could experience grace (see Heb. 12:1-4). We are called to walk by faith not by sight. In other words, we are called to trust in God even when we don't feel like it.

It's easy to follow Christ when all the emotions are there, isn't it? However, when we don't necessarily feel Him, or things are not necessarily going our way, it can be difficult to remain steadfast. This is when our faith is tested. We have the opportunity to become the most peculiar when things are not going well; that's when we find strength in Christ to experience true joy! James writes about this:

My brethren, count it all joy when you fall into various trials, knowing that the testing of your faith produces patience.

But let patience have its perfect work, that you may be perfect and complete, lacking nothing. If any of you lacks wisdom, let him ask of God, who gives to all liberally and
without reproach, and it will be given to him. But let him ask
in faith, with no doubting, for he who doubts is like a wave
of the sea driven and tossed by the wind. For let not that man
suppose that he will receive anything from the Lord; he is a
double-minded man, unstable in all his ways (Jas. 1:2-8).

Eve had trouble with her emotions, didn't she? She gave in to her
feelings in regard to what the tree of the knowledge of good and
evil represented. She relied on her feelings instead of trusting that
God's plan was best. *Oh, that we would use our emotions for God's glory
versus the world's.*

What Our Appearance Communicates to the World
How peculiar is your dress? Does your outward appearance reflect
a holy woman on the inside? Or does the way you dress distract
from what is most important?

It isn't always easy to be different in the way we dress, especially
in a society that takes every opportunity to engulf us into a certain
image. The world's view for a woman is to be the prettiest, the
thinnest and to reveal as much of her body as possible and still remain clothed. There are pressures all around us today to be a certain size and to dress in a very seductive way.

Do you remember the description in Proverbs 7:6-27 of the
married woman who seduced a young man? How did she allure
him? "With the attire of a harlot, and a crafty heart" (v. 10), and
"with her enticing speech she caused him to yield, with her flatter-
ing lips she seduced him" (v. 21). This young man was attracted to
this married woman's outward appearance, which only made him
think of sexual intimacy. What message do we send by the clothes,
or lack of clothes, that we wear?

If you are not remaining steadfast in walking out your true identity, you will grow discontent in your walk with God. When you are

not growing in your walk with Christ, you will seek to gain the attention of others. When you forget that you are accepted by God and have all you need in Him, you seek to gain your security and identity in other directions, just as this woman dressed as a harlot.

Many of us say we have a new identity, but we dress in a way that reflects the world. To remain steadfast in living out our true identity, we must see our value and worth as women.

I will never forget what my brother Jeremy shared with his youth group on one occasion: "Don't advertise what's not for sale." You may think something is just "cute," but if it is revealing areas of your body that bring too much attention to your outward shell (skin), rather than the inward adornment of your heart, then you shouldn't wear it. Because we are God's temple, even the clothes we wear can distract someone from Christ or fail to reflect our inward beauty.

I don't know about you, but I want others to see my inward beauty. Paul instructs us in 1 Timothy 2:9-10 to focus more on our inward attributes than our outward adornment: "In like manner also, that the women adorn themselves in modest apparel, with propriety and moderation, not with braided hair or gold or pearls or costly clothing, but, which is proper for women professing godliness, with good works."

Eve had trouble with her dress, didn't she? She was clothed with the righteousness of God and experienced true contentment, having access to everything she could possibly desire. But after she sinned against God, she tried to cover herself with fig leaves. She literally sought to hide from God. *Oh, that we would dress for His glory versus the world's.*

The true secret to remaining steadfast in our commitment to living out our true identity is found in James 1:22-25:

> But be doers of the word, and not hearers only, deceiving yourselves. For if anyone is a hearer of the word and not a doer, he is like a man observing his natural face in a mirror; for he observes himself, goes away, and immediately forgets what kind of man he was. But he who looks into

the perfect law of liberty and continues in it, and is not a forgetful hearer but a doer of the work, this one will be blessed in what he does.

The key phrase here is "continues in it." This is what it means to remain steadfast. In order to be His peculiar woman, you must remain connected to the greatest Source: Christ Jesus. Another word for "connected" is "abide." We learn a lot about abiding in Christ in John 15:4: "Abide in Me, and I in you. As the branch cannot bear fruit of itself, unless it abides in the vine, neither can you, unless you abide in Me."

We need so desperately to be growing in our relationship with Christ on a daily basis. As our relationship goes ever deeper with our Maker, we will reflect Him because we know Him, and we will be able to stand when things get tough.

Let's not just hear the Word, but let's also apply its truths to our lives each and every day.

Listen to God's Voice

Spending time in God's Word every day has helped me the most to grow in my walk with Him. You may already do this. Perhaps you have a devotional book with Scripture in it that helps you understand what God's Word says. Regardless, you must also saturate yourself with the Word to deflect the many lies you will encounter everywhere you go.

Before you begin reading the Word of God, ask the Lord to cleanse your life from anything that would hinder you from hearing His voice, and then to help you understand what He is saying. So many times the Holy Spirit has convicted me of things in my life that I need to repent of before I begin reading Scripture.

I also try to memorize Scripture. We read in Psalm 119:11, "Your word I have hidden in my heart, that I might not sin against You." As you treasure His Word and cherish the path He has for you, it will keep you from sin. I have been in many places or involved in conversations with people when a verse of Scripture has come to mind that I have memorized. It has helped me in those situations, and I know it will help you in your walk with God too.

Besides reading the Scriptures daily, learning to communicate with my Creator has been the greatest blessing in my life. Spending time in prayer is imperative for any believer to know and experience God. Paul wrote in 1 Thessalonians 5:17, "Pray without ceasing." Talking with your Creator God should be a natural part of your day-by-day, moment-by-moment lifestyle. Jesus specifically told us in Matthew 28:20 that He is always with us. And we read in Deuteronomy 31:6-8:

> "Be strong and of good courage, do not fear nor be afraid of them; for the LORD your God, He is the One who goes with you. He will not leave you nor forsake you." Then Moses called Joshua and said to him in the sight of all Israel, "Be strong and of good courage, for you must go with this people to the land which the LORD has sworn to their fathers to give them, and you shall cause them to inherit it. And the LORD, He is the One who goes before you. He will be with you, He will not leave you nor forsake you; do not fear nor be dismayed."

God is concerned about everything in your life. You have the privilege to talk to Him about anything, at any time. You don't need to set up an appointment or schedule a meeting with Him. He is always here for you. As you learn to open up to Him and talk with Him, you will also learn to be quiet and still and allow Him to teach you and minister to you through His living Word.

Respond to God's Voice

When I first came to Christ, I began to keep a prayer journal. I recorded my prayers and thoughts to God. This has helped me in my prayer life. I am able to go back in my journals and see how God has answered prayer and helped me through difficult seasons in my life. Perhaps this would help you too.

Often, God calls us to pray intentionally for a specific need by fasting. Fasting simply means to do without something for a period of time. It could be deciding not to watch television for a few days or going without a meal, all for the purpose of devoting your heart and mind to reflect and pray on a specific need.

When Queen Esther did not know how deliverance was going to come for her people, the Jews, she called for them to fast for three days: "Then Esther told them to reply to Mordecai: 'Go, gather all the Jews who are present in Shushan, and fast for me; neither eat nor drink for three days, night or day. My maids and I will fast likewise. And so I will go to the king, which is against the law; and if I perish, I perish!'" (Esther 4:15-16).

During her fast, Esther was convinced of how she was to go before King Ahasuerus and gain his favor. Prayer through fasting not only displays our faith in God, but it also reveals our desperate cry to hear from Him, the only one who can make a difficult situation into something beautiful.

As you enter into prayer on a daily basis and read the Scriptures, you are called to respond to the Word of God. The Scriptures are alive and active and always call for a response. We have the choice to obey or disobey; to surrender our lives in worship or to walk in deception. "All Scripture is given by inspiration of God, and is profitable for doctrine, for reproof, for correction, for instruction in righteousness, that the man of God may be complete, thoroughly equipped for every good work" (2 Tim. 3:16-17). As we seek to reflect Him and mirror His image, we will obey Him at any cost, because He can be trusted and His way is always best.

Ask yourself this question: "If Jesus came back today, would He find a peculiar woman in me?" When we reflect His image, we become more than meets the eye. Oh, that others would see Christ in us as we live out our true identity and remain steadfast in our commitment to obey Him!

I remember being challenged with becoming steadfast in my own devotion to living out my true identity. I knew God knew my heart and could understand me more than I could understand myself, so I just began to talk to Him about it. The exact prayer I communicated to Him is written below. At the end of the prayer, He reminded me of the joy I had in Him and the plans He had for His peculiar daughter. I pray it will be an encouragement to you.

Your calling, dear LORD, is more vital than anything I know. It is higher than any dream or expectation. It draws me into the secret place to engage in the sweetest conversation one could ever imagine.

Your calling, oh LORD, makes me peculiar. It separates me from things that I would have formerly enjoyed.

Your calling, dear LORD, brings to me the highest responsibility and accountability, yet it is the greatest privilege in which You have allowed me to engage!

Your calling, oh LORD, is one of which I am not worthy. There is nothing in and of me that makes this calling; it is simply the great work You are accomplishing through a simple girl who has made herself available.

Yet, who would not dare to give themselves to the Maker of the sky, the seas and the mountains?

Who would think about hesitating to give themselves completely under the daily Lordship of Christ?

Yet, we all, somehow, somewhere, and sometime . . . hesitate again, being deceived into believing we are masters of our own lives and must be in control.

May this simple girl simply trust in You . . . that is faith . . . that is growth . . . that is giving complete access to You, dear LORD, to have Your will and way in me and allowing You freedom to ac-complish the calling You have placed upon me.

The Way to Remain Steadfast

- Always remember who you are and what it means to be His peculiar woman.
- Do not be ashamed of who you are as His peculiar woman.
- Gain your strength from Christ when you are tested, persecuted and tempted.
- Seek Him daily in the Scriptures and in prayer.
- Obey Him and trust that His way is best.

Dear God,
Make me into Your peculiar woman. May I live a life for Your glory and remain steadfast in my commitment to live out my true identity. Enable me to reflect Your image in all I say and do. Help me to seek You daily and obey You, knowing that Your way is the best. In Your name I pray, amen.

YOUR PRAYER

_____
_____
_____
_____
_____
_____
_____
_____
_____
_____
_____
_____
_____
_____

What Do You Think?

Why is it important to remain steadfast in living out your true identity?

_____

_____

_____

_____

_____

_____

How can you remain steadfast in living out your true identity?

_____

_____

_____

_____

_____

Do you consider yourself a peculiar woman? If so, why, and in what ways?

_____

_____

_____

_____

_____

What does it mean to reflect the image of God?

_____

_____

_____

_____

_____

Differentiate between the world's view of beauty and God's view of beauty.

_____

_____

_____

_____

_____

Do you believe that others see an "incorruptible beauty" in you? If so, how is that possible?

_____

_____

_____

_____

_____

How can you grow in your walk with God and live out your true identity?

_____

_____

_____

_____

Do you think you could honestly say to others what the apostle Paul said in 1 Corinthians 11:1—"Imitate me, just as I also imitate Christ"? If yes, in what ways do others see Christ in you? If no, would you like others to be able to follow you as an example of one who reflects the character of Christ? What areas of your life need to be reexamined and surrendered to Christ?

_____

_____

_____

_____

Unchanging Truths to Read and Treasure

PSALM 119:11
PROVERBS 7:6-27; 17:24; 18:15
JOHN 1:1-5; 2:15
1 CORINTHIANS 3:9-17
2 CORINTHIANS 4:6,16-18
PHILIPPIANS 4:8-9
1 TIMOTHY 2:9-10
2 TIMOTHY 3:16-17
JAMES 1:2-8,22-25; 3:5-12
1 PETER 2:9,11-12,21-25; 3:1-4

CHAPTER EIGHT

Radical *Ezer*— A Life that Impacts

Helping Others Take Off Their Masks

Go therefore and make disciples of all nations, baptizing them in the name of the Father and of the Son and of the Holy Spirit, teaching them to observe all things that I have commanded you; and lo, I am with you always, even to the end of the age.
MATTHEW 28:19-20

But sanctify the Lord God in your hearts, and always be ready to give a defense to everyone who asks you a reason for the hope that is in you, with meekness and fear.
1 PETER 3:15

One summer, I had the opportunity to travel to the country of Peru on a missions trip. I will never forget the 10-hour bus ride on the edge of the Andes Mountains. How beautiful the countryside was, but how incredibly bumpy and uncomfortable the journey! However, it was definitely worth it all.

A team from the United States, including myself, had been asked to visit a people group who had only heard portions of the gospel of Jesus Christ. Those who had placed their faith in Christ had not received much encouragement or teaching from the Scriptures on how to grow in their faith. I was asked to teach the Scriptures specifically to the Peruvian women at a ladies conference.

I remember preparing the Bible studies and spending a lot of time in prayer, asking the Lord to do a work in the lives of these women and use me as His vessel. My prayer was for the women to see Christ reflected in my life and, as a result, desire to know Him more and walk in their newly found identity. I also prayed that these women would truly see how valuable they were in the eyes of God, how much their Creator loved them, and that they would surrender to His plan for their lives.

I found out later that many of the women were viewed as being second-class citizens. Many were taught that only salvation was available to men. You should have seen the hope in their eyes as I taught on Galatians 3:28: "There is neither Jew nor Greek, there is neither slave nor free, there is neither male nor female; for you are all one in Christ Jesus." Regardless of race, background or gender, salvation is available for all who place their trust in the Son of God, confessing their sin and repenting from their former lifestyle. You may have never questioned this truth; however, there are many women in other regions of the world who have never heard that salvation is available to them as women. You should have seen the joy in the faces of these Peruvian women when they heard this truth.

The entire mission trip was a very humbling experience as I realized the intense hunger and desire these precious women had for the truth. The place where we met was packed with women from the village during every session. Two other ladies and I taught five to seven sessions a day for one hour each and had a captive audience every time. If we had not taught for at least one hour, the Peruvian ladies would have thought something was wrong. It was normal to spend one to two hours each teaching session.

After one of the sessions, several women came up to us wailing, with tears falling down their cheeks. We called for the interpreter to see what was wrong and asked to understand their specific need. These women were expressing deep sorrow in their spirits because they did not know how to read. We had been teaching them the importance of the Word of God and the rich truths found in Scripture. They voiced their deep desire to live out the Scriptures and teach their children principles from God's Word. At the same time, they were grieved because they could not read God's Word for themselves. Their question to us was regarding how they could teach their children if they didn't know how to read the Scriptures themselves.

We encouraged them to memorize the Scriptures we were teaching and to hide those truths in their hearts and then share His precepts with their children. I will never forget their deep-rooted desire to become godly wives and mothers.

After praying with those dear Peruvian women, we took a 30-minute break and then I was up teaching again. I began to teach a session on evangelism and how to share your faith. I had all of my notes typed up in front of me and was teaching with much fervor from God's Word. As I spoke on the necessity of sharing our faith and being His witness from the Great Commission, the words of which are found in Matthew 28:19, I noticed several young women sitting across the street. There were no doors where I was teaching, so you could see a lot of what was going on in the village.

There was a bar directly across from where I was teaching, and three girls came out of the bar and were sitting on a small cart used for their transportation. As I began to close the session and have prayer with the Christian Peruvian women, my heart became burdened for the girls across the street. I hesitated at first and thought,

I can't go over there; I am here to teach these women in this room, not to go across the street. Immediately after I hesitated, I fell under great conviction. It was as if the Lord was saying, "Monica, listen to what you are thinking . . . you are called to go everywhere and be My disciple." There was no question about it, I knew the Lord wanted me to go over and witness to the girls who had come out of the bar.

I immediately grabbed by Bible, a few gospel tracts written in their language and asked for the interpreter to go with me. I also asked the Lord to forgive me for being hesitant. How could I teach others how to share their faith if I wasn't willing to share mine? We hurried across the street. I soon realized they worked in this bar. They were dressed in a very promiscuous and seductive manner and looked at me with eyes of hopelessness. I introduced myself and tried to enter into a conversation with them. They were very open and receptive as I began to go directly into the gospel and share with them why I was there.

It was evident they had never heard of Jesus Christ. Paul wrote in Romans 10:14-15, "How then shall they call on Him in whom they have not believed? And how shall they believe in Him of whom they have not heard? And how shall they hear without a preacher? And how shall they preach unless they are sent? As it is written: 'How beautiful are the feet of those who preach the gospel of peace, who bring glad tidings of good things!'" I knew that God desired me to share His love with these young girls.

As I began to witness to them, praying at the same time that they would receive Christ, several of the men who owned the bar came outside. These men most assuredly controlled these young women. Who knows what they were forced to do, but it was obvious that these young girls had no freedom of their own. The men yelled at them to go back inside immediately. The girls looked at me as if to say, "We want to stay and listen, but we cannot." I placed tracts in their hands and yelled out, "I will be back here tomorrow at this same time and would like to finish sharing with you what we have been talking about." They nodded their heads and rushed back inside the bar.

Later that evening, I shared with the other team members what had happened and asked them to start praying for the salvation of these young women. I so desperately desired their eyes to be opened to truth and for them to know their identity in Christ. I felt for sure they would be there the next day at the same time and place. After all, I had prayed and the entire team was praying for their salvation. I could not wait to share with them.

The next day finally came, and I ran over to where they had been sitting the previous day, but they were not there. I waited for as long as I could and began to pray for them. I waited up to the point when I knew I was scheduled to teach again. I went back across the street and began to teach another session to the Peruvian women who had gathered for our last day.

To my surprise, in the middle of the teaching session, a little boy interrupted the teaching by running inside the room and yelling out, "We are waiting on you to share your story; please come and share your story with us." The interpreter turned to me and told me what this little boy had said. The boy looked to be about eight years old. *What was he talking about?* I wondered.

Little did I know that as I yelled to the girls at the bar, "I will be back here tomorrow at this same time, and would like to finish sharing with you what we have been talking about," several children riding their bicycles through the village had heard me. The girls may not have returned, but God still had a plan for me to witness and share my faith.

After you place your trust in Christ and begin walking out your true identity, Christ has given you a mission to help others take off their masks. You have the privilege of introducing your marvelous Maker to the people He places in your path. You do not necessarily choose people to witness to. God is the one who directs your steps and places specific people along the way: "A man's heart plans his way, but the LORD directs his steps" (Prov. 16:9).

I had definitely planned my way on this mission trip. I believed I knew the audience God wanted me to teach and with whom to share my faith. I sure was wrong! God definitely had other plans.

He desires that we simply make ourselves available and be ready to share whenever He places people in our path: "But sanctify the Lord God in your hearts, and always be ready to give a defense to everyone who asks you a reason for the hope that is in you, with meekness and fear" (1 Pet. 3:15).

This little eight-year-old boy and an interpreter led me across the dirt roads of the village and up onto the roof of a house. I climbed the fragile stairs and was greeted by the beautiful faces of 30 Peruvian children. These were boys and girls from 4 to 12, all sitting down in a circle, waiting for me to share a story with them. I knew immediately that I was to share the story of Christ. Most assuredly, it is the greatest story you could ever tell!

I began with the birth of Christ and tried to cover as much information as I possibly could so they would understand the gospel. I shared with the children how they could know God and how deeply He loved them. Then I asked them if they had ever heard this story. Assuming that some of them had, I was shocked to realize this was the first time any of them had heard the gospel. All of them stood to their feet to indicate they wanted a relationship with Christ. I led them in a prayer where they confessed their sins before God and asked Christ to come into their lives!

I left that roof knowing there were about 30 little brothers and little sisters in Christ that I would see in heaven. We were now part of the same family! Paul wrote in Ephesians 3:14-15, "For this reason I bow my knees to the Father of our Lord Jesus Christ, from whom the whole family in heaven and earth is named." These Peruvian children had entered into a relationship with their Maker, and I had the privilege of pointing them to Christ! They were no longer living life with masks on, alienated from God. Now they were part of His family.

And you, who once were alienated and enemies in your mind by wicked works, yet now He has reconciled in the body of His flesh through death, to present you holy, and blameless, and above reproach in His sight (Col. 1:21-22).

We Are to Help Others Find Their True Identity in Christ

Our mission as women who know their identity in Christ is to share with others how they too can have a relationship with their Maker. There are so many people who do not know their identity due to a wrong view of God.

How are we to lead others to Christ? God's Word says, "For it is the God who commanded light to shine out of darkness, who has shone in our hearts to give the light of the knowledge of the glory of God in the face of Jesus Christ" (2 Cor. 4:6). The same Maker of the universe we read about in Genesis 1-2 is the same God who has changed our lives. He has shone in our hearts so that we will then be a light—a reflection of the glory of God—to others. We are His reflection as we mirror His image.

The last part of this verse is so important! It refers to "the face of Jesus Christ." When we think of a person's face, immediately the outward image comes to mind, especially in the culture we live in today that focuses so much on the outward appearance. However, the meaning of "face" here is quite the opposite. To be the "face of Jesus Christ" is to be a reflection of our Maker. We are to mirror His image; His inward characteristics. I desire to reflect the identity of Christ and to help others take off their masks. Don't you?

The Mission of Helping Others #1: Purpose

How do we help others take off their masks? First of all, we must recognize our purpose in God's plan. Our Creator has designed each of us for a purpose. He has created us to first know Him and then to make Him known. When we understand more fully His identity and we trust in Him, He changes our lives and makes us more like Him. The purpose He has given us is to share with others about Him, just as I shared with the different people He placed in my path on the mission trip to Peru.

As we have already discussed, you are no accident or mistake. He has created you for a special purpose, to make His truth known.

He desires to use your entire personality to bring Him glory and to help others take off their masks!

I will never forget reading the story of Amy Carmichael, missionary to India. I have been greatly inspired by her writings that reflect her passion for Christ. As a young girl, she prayed that God would change the color of her eyes. She had brown eyes but preferred the color blue. Amy made this a serious matter of prayer, believing that God could and would answer this specific petition. Night and day, she made this request, but her eye color never changed. At the age of 18, she responded to missionary call and left her home in Ireland. She would soon realize that one of the reasons God had created her with brown eyes instead of blue was for the purpose of rescuing teenage girls out of temple prostitution in India.

One by one, she would rescue these young girls from the Hindu temple, sharing with each one the gospel of Jesus Christ. This was not an easy endeavor, to say the least. In fact, Amy had to actually disguise herself as an Indian woman. She wore an Indian Sari and turned her pale white skin to tan by mixing coffee grains and rubbing this all over her body. However, if her eyes had been any other color than brown, her disguise would have been discovered immediately!

God always has a purpose for everything He does. He desires to use each of us to fulfill the purpose of making Him known. He created your personality, abilities, talents, gifts and even your outward appearance to be used by Him for His purposes. Let us never forget that God has created us uniquely to help others take off their masks and assume their true identity in Christ.

In recognizing our purpose to help others take off their masks, we must understand that God's mission for us is a calling and a commission. Our commission is found in Matthew 28:19-20: "Go therefore and make disciples of all nations, baptizing them in the name of the Father and of the Son and of the Holy Spirit, teaching them to observe all things that I have commanded you; and lo, I am with you always, even to the end of the age." We are called to go and make disciples. In other words, to share Christ with others and help others know Him more. Statistics reveal that not many believers actually share their faith. When we fail to communicate God's truth to others, we are disobeying His command to go and share.

One Sunday after church, a young college student approached me and shared how she felt called to work with women in ministry but did not feel called to evangelize (share her faith). I looked up at her and said, "Oh, you are definitely called to evangelize." From the look on her face, I believe I shocked her with my immediate response.

We discussed how God's commission for all believers is to go and tell others about Him. It is not an option for the believer. My dear friend went on to share with me how she was just so scared to share her faith. She desired to do it, but then she would become filled with worry about what to say or how others would respond. Often, we may be afraid of what others may think of us if we share with them how they can have their identity in Christ. However, we must not forget that His grace is sufficient and will enable us to fulfill His purposes, in spite of ourselves.

The apostle Paul refers to this truth in 2 Corinthians 12. He had a "thorn in the flesh." We cannot be certain what "thorn" Paul asked the Lord to remove from him. However, God reminded Paul that He would be his strength in the midst of his weaknesses: "And He said to me, 'My grace is sufficient for you, for My strength is made perfect in weakness.' Therefore most gladly I will rather boast in my infirmities, that the power of Christ may rest upon me. Therefore I take pleasure in infirmities, in reproaches, in needs, in persecutions, in distresses, for Christ's sake. For when I am weak, then I am strong" (2 Cor. 12:9-10).

As we recognize our purpose from God, we must never forget that He is the one who goes before us and will give us strength to fulfill His will and His dream for our lives. Let Christ be your strength!

Remember how He enabled me as I went across the street to share with the Peruvian girls sitting outside a bar? I hesitated out of fear, but the Lord gave me confidence. When we fulfill His purpose for us, He enables us and gives us strength that casts out fear.

Be a Radical *Ezer*

Perhaps the greatest impact ever seen in Scripture would be when Jesus had just risen from the dead to prove that He was the real deal! The first individuals to see Jesus were women. He had already impacted them by His life. Now they were grieving His loss and actually had a conversation with Him, without realizing at first who He was. When they realized it was their Lord, they ran to tell the disciples! They could not hold it in! They had just seen Jesus and had to spread the news to everyone that He was real! He was alive!

Why do we hold back from sharing with others about the one we say is real and alive? We were created to know our Creator God and to impact others by sharing the truth about Him! As others see Christ reflected in our lives, they will be impacted and influenced to know Him as well.

What a purpose God has given us as women! We are called to point others to Christ! How radically we are being used of God! To be His radical *ezer* simply means to live out our purpose as women. *Ezer* is the Hebrew word for helper. As Genesis 1–3 teaches us, we are called to be helpers. Just as Christ is our helper (and the Helper of all of humanity when He laid down His life to buy our salvation), we are called to help others see their need for Him.

Are you asking yourself, *How do I fulfill God's purpose for me?* Paul gives us the answer in 2 Corinthians 4:16: "Therefore we do not lose heart. Even though our outward man is perishing, yet the inward man is being renewed day by day." It is so important to be reminded that we need to concentrate on growing inwardly (spending time in prayer and in the Scriptures) more than focusing outwardly on the body God has given us.

To most effectively help people take off their masks, we must always be ready to give an answer of what Christ has done in our life. Your life story can have an incredible impact on someone else, because no one can ever disagree with your personal story.

I was returning some books to the library of the college I once attended and ran into a young woman who had no idea who she was in Christ, but she so desperately wanted to know. After listening to her talk for a while, I asked her what she believed in. We entered a lengthy conversation about God. My friend had grown up in a religious home but had not placed her faith in Christ. I began to share my story with her and how Christ could change her life as well.

I quickly ran to my car to get my Bible, and then we looked through the Scriptures together and my friend began to understand the gospel for the first time. I asked her if she would like to have a relationship with Christ and she said yes. God's purpose for our lives is to share with others His truth. *Have you recognized and acted upon that purpose given to you from God?*

The Mission of Helping Others #2: Surrender

The second way we can help others take off their masks is to make ourselves available to be used of God in any way. In one word: surrender. We must realize that once we have placed our faith in Christ, we are called to take up our cross daily and follow Him (see Luke 9:25). Part of taking up our cross is to remind our flesh that it has been crucified and ask Christ for strength to live each day His way and not our own way. We must surrender to His plan and purposes.

In Ephesians 3:20-21, Paul reminds us that God's plan always exceeds our plan. His dream for our lives is always better than what we could ask for or imagine: "Now to Him who is able to do exceedingly abundantly above all that we ask or think, according to the power that works in us, to Him be glory in the church by Christ Jesus to all generations, forever and ever." He is able to fulfill His purpose through us, but we must surrender to Him daily and submit to His plan. As we make ourselves available to God, we are literally saying, "Whatever, whenever, wherever, however, whoever." It is not for us to decide where we want to go and serve or even who we want to help. As God opens up the doors, we are to walk through them.

As I was preparing for my first mission trip overseas to the country of India, I battled with whether or not God wanted me to go. I felt so weak and small. I kept thinking of other people who would be better candidates for missionary work. I didn't feel like I had anything significant to offer. The Lord reminded me that I had surrendered to Him. He also reminded me that I had nothing to offer in and of myself, but with Him, I had everything to offer! I had truth to proclaim to these people who were blinded by the world and Satan.

I began to pray every day, "Whatever Your purpose, Lord, whenever Your timing, wherever the place, whoever the people, however the plan," and I meant it with all my heart.

The Lord reminded me that although I was a small light, even a little light will shine in the darkness. He confirmed in my heart that I was to go to India on this mission trip and He would work through me because I had surrendered to His plan. I am so glad I surrendered, because I had the privilege of witnessing the Lord do amazing things!

One of the first meetings we had in India was a women's conference. The room was filled with around 350 Indian women. Most of the women were widows between the ages of 16 to 25. Due to tribal warfare, many of the women had lost their husbands at a very young age. I began to share from the Scriptures on the worth and value of women. After the session concluded, a young Indian woman approached me. She was one of the very few who spoke English, and she spoke it well. I later learned that she was a young college student who had heard that someone from America was speaking. She was also a Hindu.

I remember her sharing with me how the message had inspired her. She then went on to say that she wanted to know how to accept the God I was talking about. She already worshiped many other gods. We sat there and talked for a very long time about Christ being the only way to Father God. This dear young woman was so blinded to this truth. I invited her to come to another session and she did. I began to pray that the Lord would open her spiritual eyes. After the second session, she stayed afterward to talk again. I shared with her how she could know Christ and how He was the only true and living God. I also shared with her many verses in Scripture that spoke to her heart.

I was filled with joy when she said she wanted to become a Christian. We sat there on the pew of the church and she prayed to ask Christ into her life! I was so thrilled to help my new sister take off her mask.

When we surrender daily to the will of God, He will open doors to share with others. *Have you made yourself available to be used of God?* Remember: "Whatever Your purpose, Lord, whenever Your timing, wherever the place, whoever the people, however the plan."

The Mission of Helping Others #3: Living the Truth

The third way to help others take off their mask is to live the truth. This is the most powerful way to make a true impact. When you live out your true identity, you will make a difference in the lives of others: "For we are His workmanship, created in Christ Jesus for good works, which God prepared beforehand that we should walk in them" (Eph. 2:10). It is one thing to proclaim the truth, but it's a completely different thing to live out the truth. We are called to live out what we proclaim.

I remember not having many close friends in high school. It was a constant struggle for me. I never belonged to a "clique" or a specific "group." I decided to be friends with everyone but didn't really have many close relationships.

I desired to be used of God, and I remember praying each day before I left for high school that the Lord would help me be His light and live for Him. I was never invited to any of the parties or social events. People knew that I was a Christian, and I really did stand for the Lord in the strength He gave me.

Monica Rose Brennan · www.regalbooks.com

One day, I saw a young girl run down the steps into the bathroom. I could tell she was crying. I knew who she was, and she knew who I was, but she never wanted to hang around me much because I was a Christian. I immediately felt burdened to go and see what was wrong. I ran to the girls' restroom and found her literally sobbing. When she looked up at me, I placed my arm around her and asked her what was wrong.

She shared with me how she hated herself and had tried to commit suicide the night before but didn't succeed. She told me she was going to try again. I began to share with her how special she was in the eyes of God and how He loved her so much. There in the restroom she prayed and asked Christ to come into her life. Although my friend never wanted to hang out with me before this, because I was a Christian, when times got tough she knew she could open up to me. Why? I had lived out the truth in front of her. Our impact is the greatest when others both hear the truth and see it lived out in front of them. *Are you proclaiming truth by living out the truth?*

The Mission of Helping Others #4: Pleasing God

The fourth way we can help others take off their mask is to live to please God and God alone. As others see the difference He has made in our lives and how our focus is on pleasing Him, they will see the truth lived out. We must be willing to stand for Christ regardless of what others say or think of us.

> Therefore we make it our aim, whether present or absent, to be well pleasing to Him. For we must all appear before the judgment seat of Christ, that each one may receive the things *done* in the body, according to what he has done, whether good or bad. Knowing, therefore, the terror of the Lord, we persuade men; but we are well known to God, and I also trust are well known in your consciences (2 Cor. 5:9-11).

We will be judged based on what we have done in pointing others to Christ. If we live to please Him, He will manifest Himself through our lives and others will be drawn to Him. *Are you living a life that pleases God and God alone?*

The greatest way we can embark on God's mission in helping others take off their masks is to daily remind ourselves of who we are in Christ and submit to His will. As we recognize our purpose, make ourselves available to be used of God, proclaim His truth by living out the truth and live to please God and God alone, others will take off their masks and gain their true identity in Christ. We cannot take off the masks from anyone, but we can live a life that draws them to God and His saving grace.

The Mandate: Equipping Others

Christ has not only called us to embark on His mission, but He has also given us a mandate to follow. We are to be His witnesses, but that's not all. He desires that we equip others to grow deeper in their walk with God. After we discover our true identity, we are called to help others discover theirs.

The apostle Paul tells us, in Titus 2:3-5, how we are to equip other women in their walk with God. Paul reminds the spiritually mature woman of who she is and how she is to reach out to help other women. It is vital for any Christian woman desiring to make a true impact on others to be in the Scriptures and in communication with her Maker on a consistent, daily basis.

The Spiritually Mature Woman

There are certain character qualities that should be present in any Christian woman, especially the woman who desires to influence others: "The older women likewise, that they be reverent in behavior, not slanderers, not given to much wine, teachers of good things" (Titus 2:3). To be a woman of spiritual influence, your lifestyle should be different than someone who is not a Christian.

You can possess a desire to influence others but not make an eternal impact if your lifestyle is contrary to what Paul is exhorting the Christian woman to be. As we walk with Christ, He produces more and more change in our lives.

The spiritually mature Christian woman cannot possess these qualities apart from Christ. He is the one who produces the character. In these verses from Titus 2, we are first reminded to be reverent in behavior. This would include my speech, my dress, my attitude, my actions and my reactions. When others see you, do they see someone they can follow? Someone who is being molded more into the image of God every day? Or do they see someone who is a follower of culture and being molded more into the image of the world every day? Only you can answer these questions.

You are not ready to influence others effectively if you haven't surrendered your entire demeanor to Christ's influence. Perhaps you struggle with this. Ask the Lord to help you in this area of your life. If your demeanor doesn't reflect Christ, then instead of being a help to others, you can become a hindrance.

Watch Your Words
The woman of influence is also reminded not to be slanderous. To be slanderous would include gossip or cutting through another woman's character. This would also include saying things about a woman who doesn't have her identity in Christ. As influencers, we are called not to judge others but to love them and meet them at the point of their need. If we are judging them, then this would be a barrier in our influence of them.

We often have a tendency to try to "conform" them into a certain image we believe they should become, instead of allowing the Lord to "transform" their lives. An effective influencer will pray for the transformation of the person who needs Christ and will not seek to mold her into a certain image. Paul states in Romans 12:1-2, "I beseech you therefore, brethren, by the mercies of God, that you present your bodies a living sacrifice, holy, acceptable to God, which is your reasonable service. And do not be conformed to this world, but be transformed by the renewing of your mind, that you may prove what is that good and acceptable and perfect will of God."

We must accept other women where they are in order to have an effective influence over them. I am reminded of a woman who approached a pastor's wife expressing the desire to pour her life into other women. The pastor's wife was thrilled at the zeal and desire this woman possessed. The woman went on to share how some of the women in the church were really getting on her nerves and she had no time for those types of women. The pastor's wife turned to her and said, "Then you are not ready to influence." When we are slanderous, we put up a barrier and fail to help others understand their true identity. Have you been a slanderous woman? Ask the Lord to forgive you and help you accept others at the point of their need.

Be Above Reproach

The woman of influence is also reminded to live a life above reproach and to be a teacher of good things. She is to communicate the Word of God but also live it out in front of others. She should be living a life free from addictions and bondage.

When I was struggling with anorexia, I was not at a point where I should have been influencing anyone. My life had a lot of bondage in it. I was the one in need of being influenced. When I got better and was free from bondage, I had the opportunity to spend time with other girls who were struggling in the same way I once did. I was able to offer them hope and share with them how they could be healed completely with the help of Christ. Have you struggled with an addiction or bondage? Ask the Lord to help you overcome these barriers so you can effectively influence others.

After looking at the character traits a woman of influence should possess to impact other women and help them discover their identity, the apostle Paul exhorts the older women to admonish the younger women "to love their husbands, to love their children, to be discreet, chaste, homemakers, good, obedient to their own husbands, that the word of God may not be blasphemed" (Titus 2:4-5). The spiritually mature woman is given the mandate to teach the younger woman how to love her husband and children sacrificially. They are also to teach them how to be discreet and how to value their home and family. What an impact an older woman can have on a younger woman!

A woman of influence can also have a negative effect on another woman if she forgets who she is as described in verse 3 and starts walking in a direction that is the opposite of her true identity. Examples: being judgmental, gossiping, demonstrating rude behavior (the opposite of being kind) and hypocrisy. Although no one is perfect, there should be a certain stability of conduct (walking in right relationship with Christ) for the woman who knows her identity in Christ and influences others.

Love

The most effective way to influence others is to love. This is most assuredly the mark of true Christian maturity. A biblical definition of love is found in 1 Corinthians 13:1-13:

> Though I speak with the tongues of men and of angels, but have not love, I have become a sounding brass or a clanging cymbal. And though I have the gift of prophecy, and understand all mysteries and all knowledge, and though I have all faith, so that I could remove mountains, but have not love, I am nothing. And though I bestow all my goods to feed the poor, and though I give my body to be burned, but have not love, it profits me nothing.
>
> Love suffers long and is kind; love does not envy; love does not parade itself, is not puffed up; does not behave rudely, does not seek its own, is not provoked, thinks no evil; does not rejoice in iniquity, but rejoices in the truth; bears all things, believes all things, hopes all things, endures all things.

Love never fails. But whether there are prophecies, they will fail; whether there are tongues, they will cease; whether there is knowledge, it will vanish away. For we know in part and we prophesy in part. But when that which is perfect has come, then that which is in part will be done away.

When I was a child, I spoke as a child, I understood as a child, I thought as a child; but when I became a man, I put away childish things. For now we see in a mirror, dimly, but then face to face. Now I know in part, but then I shall know just as I also am known. And now abide faith, hope, love, these three; but the greatest of these is love.

Regardless of personality, struggles, economic status, race or background, we are called to love people. Christ is our prime example of true love as He laid down His life for us, in spite of our sins. "And above all things have fervent love for one another, for 'love will cover a multitude of sins'" (1 Pet. 4:8). A woman can make the greatest impact on others when she not only accepts others, no matter what, but as she models in front of them the love of Christ, no matter what. The goodness of God is what leads us to repentance. As we model the essence of who our Maker is, others will see His love through us. As Paul writes:

Therefore you are inexcusable, O man, whoever you are who judge, for in whatever you judge another you condemn yourself; for you who judge practice the same things. But we know that the judgment of God is according to truth against those who practice such things. And do you think this, O man, you who judge those practicing such things, and doing the same, that you will escape the judgment of God? Or do you despise the riches of His goodness, forbearance, and longsuffering, not knowing that the goodness of God leads you to repentance? (Rom. 2:1-4).

Acceptance

So many young women I meet with on a regular basis have expressed a fear of opening up with another woman about their past. The fear of being rejected can keep women who desire to be set free in great bondage. There are so many women who desire to know their identity and to walk without a mask, but they are afraid to confide in another person. There is no room for judgment when you are seeking to make an eternal impact on someone. We are all in need of Christ, and women desperately need other women to help point them to their Maker.

I have learned so much about influencing others from my mother. I would not only refer to her as the model pastor's wife, but also as a true Christian woman. To this day, I've never met anyone who has a more intense passion for pointing others to Christ. Several years ago, she and my father were visiting a church my father had formerly pastored. An older lady approached her, overwhelmed with joy to see her again. As my mother embraced her with open arms, this poor widowed woman whispered in my mother's ear, "Thank you for always loving me. You are the only pastor's wife I have had that didn't treat me like I was contaminated." If we desire to make a true impact, we must see people as our Maker sees them: beautiful. My mother impacted this dear lady by loving her as Christ loved her. Are you loving others with the power of Christ's love?

Proverbs 29:18 says, "Where there is no revelation, the people cast off restraint; but happy is he who keeps the law." True impact will always include being a woman of vision. If we desire to help others take off their masks, then we must make them aware of their worth to God and their purpose given to them by God.

The Samaritan woman had relationships with many men, but Christ accepted her by sharing truth with her. Women were looked at as inferior citizens in biblical times, and even Jesus' disciples "marveled that He talked with a woman" (John 4:27). However, Christ met the woman at the point of her need. He was not thinking, *What a hopeless case; I have no time for this.* Rather, He saw a future evangelist!

Do you want to help others take off their masks and find their true identity in Christ? Then love others, accept them and see the vision God has for their lives. Our Maker so desires that we know Him and then proclaim His truth to a world mesmerized with lies.

Let's go and tell others how they can know who they are by embracing who their Maker is!

Dear God,
Please enable me to help others take off their masks.
Help me not to be afraid to share with others Your truth and to
remember that You are always with me. Help me not to care
what others think, but to live to please You. Make me into a
woman of influence. Strengthen me to impact the world for Your
glory. I surrender to Your plan. Whatever Your purpose, Lord,
whatever Your timing, wherever the place, whoever the people
and however the plan, I will trust in You.
In Your name I pray, amen.

YOUR PRAYER

_____

_____

_____

_____

_____

_____

_____

_____

_____

_____

WHAT DO YOU THINK?

Has there been anyone who has helped you take off your mask? If so, who was it, and how did this person help you take off your mask?

_____
_____
_____
_____
_____
_____

Why is it important to help others take off their masks?

_____
_____
_____
_____
_____

In what ways are you sharing God's truth with others?

_____
_____
_____
_____
_____

Have you ever been afraid to share your faith? How can you overcome this fear?

_____
_____
_____
_____
_____

List the names of people you know that need to hear the truth about God. Pray that the Lord would use you to share truth with them.

How can you effectively impact and influence others to walk in their true identity?

What are the four steps discussed in this chapter in regard to the mission of helping others take off their masks? What step(s) have you struggled with?

Describe what it means to be a woman of influence as seen in Titus 2:3-5. What are the hindrances to being a woman of influence? How can you overcome these barriers and make an eternal impact on others?

Unchanging Truths to Read and Treasure

PROVERBS 29:18
MATTHEW 28:19
ROMANS 2:1-4
1 CORINTHIANS 13
2 CORINTHIANS 4:16; 5:9-11; 12:7-10
EPHESIANS 2:10
COLOSSIANS 1:21-22
TITUS 2:3-5
1 PETER 3:15

ACKNOWLEDGMENTS

First and foremost, I would like to thank my Lord and Savior, Jesus Christ, for giving me the strength and focus to write this book. I am confident that He is the One who placed this material so heavy on my heart. It is all because of Him and for His glory.

I am so thankful for my husband, Michael Sean, whose love, support and prayers gave me freedom to spend time writing for God's glory. I am so blessed for my daughter, Elizabeth Rose, who was growing in my womb throughout a large majority of the writing of this book and who served as a constant reminder of how marvelous our Creator uniquely designs each one of us.

I am grateful for my loving father, George Rose, who has served as my pastor since I was born, faithfully teaching me the Scriptures and prayed with me to receive Christ as my personal Savior. I would like to thank my mother and greatest mentor, Nedra Rose, who read every word of the manuscript and prayed with me for women to be impacted for eternity. To my grandparents, George and Elgiva Rose, my prayer warriors, who exemplify Christlikeness more than anyone I have ever known. I would like to thank my brother, Jeremy, and his wife, Jill, as well as my nephews, J-J and Caleb, and my nieces, Bethany and Elsie Grace, whose laughter, love and prayers add so much joy to my life. I am thankful for my brother, Brady, whose passion for the Lord and integrity of life has encouraged me in writing of this book.

I am grateful to Dr. and Mrs. Elmer Towns, who continued to encourage me to get published and write for God's glory. I am thankful for the School of Religion Department at Liberty University and the professors and women's ministry students who have and continue to impact my life and inspire me to write. I am thankful for my mentor and professor, Dr. Dorothy Patterson, who taught me from the Scriptures about God's design for womanhood and pioneered programs for women on the graduate level.

I am also grateful for my mentor and close friend, Jackie Kendall, who exhorted me to stay pure and holy before God and to love Jesus more than anything.

I am so thankful for my family at Oasis Church and the women who attend our monthly WOW meetings. Their love and prayers continue to be a constant inspiration.

Last, but definitely not least, I praise the Lord for my friends at Regal who have made the publishing of this book possible. A special thanks to Bill Greig III, Stan Jantz and Kim Bangs, as well as the entire editing team. The spirit of Christlikeness and integrity is evident in all they do at Regal.

BIBLIOGRAPHY

Nee, Watchman. *The Normal Christian Life*. Fort Washington: Christian Literature Crusade, 1973.

Spurgeon, Charles H. "Commentary on Psalm 139:14." "The Treasury of David." http://bible.crosswalk.com/Commentaries/ TreasuryofDavid/tod.cgi?book=ps&chapter=139&verse=014. 1865-1885.

Tozer, A. W. *The Knowledge of the Holy*. New York: Harper Collins, 1961.

Williams, Margery. *The Velveteen Rabbit*. Tennessee: The Dalmatian Press, 1999.

About the Author

Monica Rose Brennan teaches in the School of Religion at Liberty University as Women's Ministries and Evangelism professor, serves as the Director of the Center for Women's Ministries for Liberty University, and is the founder of the Academic Program for Women's Ministries at Liberty University. With a passion for God's Word, Monica's desire is for others to discover more fully who they are in Christ in order to effectively evangelize and disciple others. Monica's more specific burden is for women to be educated, encouraged and edified by the unchanging principles found in God's Word and to become women of influence in today's secular culture by impacting their home, church and society.

Monica holds an Education degree from Wingate University, an Advanced Women's Studies certificate from Southeastern Baptist Theological Seminary, a Master of Arts in Religion degree from Liberty Baptist Theological Seminary, and a Doctorate of Ministry degree from Liberty Baptist Theological Seminary. She is a frequent speaker to teenage girls and women at youth camps and women's conferences in the United States and abroad.

Monica serves as the Women's Ministry Director at Oasis Church in Amherst, Virginia. Her husband, Dr. Michael Brennan, serves as a professor in the Center for Worship at Liberty University. They reside in Madison Heights, Virginia, and have one child.

Contact information:
email: marvelouslymade1@yahoo.com

Join the group on **Facebook**:
Marvelously Made

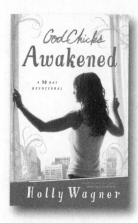

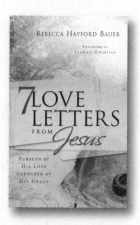
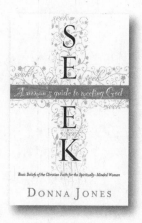